RISK

WITHDRAWN

Risk (second edition) is a fully revised and expanded update of a highly-cited, influential and well-known book. It reviews the three major approaches to risk in social and cultural theory, devoting a chapter to each one. These approaches were first identified and described by Deborah Lupton in the original edition and have since become widely used as a categorization of risk perspectives.

The first draws upon the work of Mary Douglas to articulate the 'cultural/symbolic' perspective on risk. The second approach is that of the 'risk society' perspective, based on the writings of Ulrich Beck and Anthony Giddens. The third approach explored here is that of the 'governmentality' perspective, which builds on Michel Foucault's work. Other chapters examine in detail the relationship between concepts of risk and concepts of selfhood and the body, the notion of Otherness and how this influences the ways in which people respond to and think about risk, and the pleasures of voluntary risk-taking, including discussion of edgework.

This new edition examines these themes in relation to the newly emerging threats of the twenty-first century, such as climate change, extreme weather events, terrorism and global financial crises. It will appeal to students and scholars throughout the social sciences and humanities.

Deborah Lupton is a Sociologist in the Department of Sociology and Social Policy at the University of Sydney. She is the author/ co-author of 12 books, including *Risk and Everyday Life* (2003, with John Tulloch), *Risk and Sociocultural Theory* (1999, editor), *Medicine as Culture* (2012, third edition) and *Fat* (2012). Her blog 'This Sociological Life' may be found at http://simplysociology. wordpress.com.

KEY IDEAS

Series Editor: PETER HAMILTON

Designed to complement the successful *Key Sociologists*, this series covers the main concepts, issues, debates and controversies in sociology and the social sciences. The series aims to provide authoritative essays on central topics of social science, such as community, power, work, sexuality, inequality, benefits and ideology, class, family, etc. Books adopt a strong 'individual' line, as critical essays rather than literature surveys, offering lively and original treatments of their subject matter. The books will be useful to students and teachers of sociology, political science, economics, psychology, philosophy and geography.

RISK

Second edition

Deborah Lupton

Routledge
Taylor & Francis Group
LONDON AND NEW YORK

First edition published 1999
by Routledge
Second edition published 2013
by Routledge
2 Park Square, Milton Park, Abingdon, Oxon OX14 4RN

Simultaneously published in the USA and Canada
by Routledge
711 Third Avenue, New York, NY 10017

Routledge is an imprint of the Taylor & Francis Group, an informa business

British Library Cataloguing in Publication Data
A catalogue record for this book is available from the British Library

Library of Congress Cataloging-in-Publication Data
Lupton, Deborah.
   Risk / Deborah Lupton. – 2nd ed.
     p. cm. – (Key ideas)
   Includes bibliographical references and index.
   1. Risk–Sociological aspects. 2. Risk perception–Social aspects. I. Title.
   HM1101.L87 2013
   302'.12–dc23

                                                              2012036190

ISBN: 978-0-415-62253-0 (hbk)
ISBN: 978-0-415-62254-7 (pbk)
ISBN: 978-0-203-07016-1 (ebk)

Typeset in Garamond and Scala
by Cenveo Publisher Services

Printed and bound by CPI Group (UK) Ltd, Croydon, CR0 4YY

Contents

1

INTRODUCTION

In his history of life in medieval France, Robert Muchembled (1985) portrays a world in which there were many threats and dangers to human health and life for both peasantry and aristocracy alike. During this era, death was 'on display everywhere, to the point of banality' (ibid.: 31). The most extreme of these threats and dangers were hunger, cold, epidemic disease and war. Food supply at the end of the Middle Ages in Europe was very tenuous. Grain provided the basis of the diet, and production was vulnerable to the vicissitudes of the seasons. Infant mortality was very high and lifespans short (reaching the age of 40 being considered a fair lifespan). Epidemics of such diseases as smallpox, whooping cough, typhoid, syphilis, dysentery and the plague regularly struck villages and towns, decimating their populations. People living in rural areas faced other dangers, such as wolves, which were known to attack children and sometimes adults in the fields and near their cottages. Wild dogs presented the threat of rabies should they bite and wild pigs were known to attack and eat small children. Bands of brigands roamed the forests and high roads, regularly attacking and robbing peasants. Feuds and battles between family clans were frequent and violent, often resulting in murder.

In this world, insecurity was rife and permanent, and 'fears, real and imaginary, abounded' (Muchembled 1985: 22). Dead bodies were very much in the public eye. Bodies of hanged men dangled from gallows, slowly rotting, for several days or weeks in public places, executions took place in public and the dead victims of brigands and soldiers were to be found on roads, as were the bodies of beggars and vagabonds who had perished from starvation or disease. Villagers and townspeople closed themselves in their dwellings at night, not daring to go out once darkness had fallen, because night was considered the domain of all dangers: the kingdom of the Devil, of demons, of witches and werewolves and monstrous beasts. They were also afraid of natural events that were seen to disturb the order of things, such as comets, extraordinary cold, earthquakes and floods.

In medieval France, therefore, magic, combined with a dash of Christianity, served as the belief system by which threats and dangers were dealt with conceptually and behaviourally, allowing people to feel as if they had some sense of control over their world. The presence of the supernatural was taken for granted, incorporating notions of a vengeful God with that of an evil Satan. A network of superstition existed to deal with evil, including beliefs in portents, pilgrimages to shrines, amulets, offerings to the gods, avoidance of tabooed places such as crossroads and of people such as lepers and gypsies. Everyday life was full of customs and beliefs that involved behaving in certain ways or avoiding actions so as to ward off danger or disease. Thus, for example, in some areas of France it was believed that kittens born in the month of May must be drowned, or danger would threaten (Muchembled 1985: 81).

This description of everyday life and beliefs in medieval France provides a fascinating account of how people in that particular historical and sociocultural context dealt with danger, hazard and fear. As Muchembled shows, societies develop a system of strategies and beliefs in the attempt to deal with, contain and prevent danger. To lack such systems is to throw oneself upon the mercy of fate, to relinquish any sense of control. In contemporary Western societies, where control over one's life has become increasingly viewed as important, the concept of 'risk' is now widely used to explain deviations from the norm, misfortune and frightening events. This concept assumes human responsibility and that 'something can be done' to prevent misfortune. Feelings of insecurity are common, just as they were in pre-modern times, but we now harbour somewhat different fears, different targets and causes for our anxiety. While we no longer regularly view dead bodies lying about, while the plague has all but vanished as a cause of death, while infant mortality is extremely low and most of us expect to live well into old age, we fear being the victim of a crime, falling prey to cancer, being in a car accident, losing our jobs, having our marriage break down or our children fail at school. As in pre-modern times, the symbolic basis of our uncertainties is anxiety created by disorder, the loss of control over our bodies, our relationships with others, our livelihoods and the extent to which we can exert autonomy in our everyday lives.

As in pre-modern times, we may acknowledge that threats exist, but we like to think that something can be done to deal with them. We may not perform such acts as drowning unfortunate kittens born in the wrong month as a strategy of risk prevention, but we have a range of other strategies that in emotional terms serve the same purpose. Agitating for anti-pollution legislation, watching one's diet, having tests to diagnose disease in its early stages, installing a burglar alarm in one's home, going online to seek further information or taking out life insurance are all ways in which people seek to contain and manage the anxiety and fear aroused by what they perceive to be a danger or threat. Rational thinking, bureaucratic systems of prevention, ways of identifying threats before they take effect, are regularly put forward as means of managing danger and threats.

The response to the Port Arthur killings in Australia is one example. On 28 April 1996, a young man, Martin Bryant, entered the Port Arthur historic tourist site in the Australian island state of Tasmania and proceeded to shoot randomly at people visiting and working there using two semi-automatic weapons. He then left Port Arthur and travelled to a local guest house, shooting at others and taking a male hostage en route. Bryant was not arrested until the next morning, when he ran out of the guest house after having set it alight. He had left 35 people dead and a further 17 badly wounded.

A central theme in the media coverage of the Port Arthur killings, which received a high level of publicity both in Australia and abroad, questioned why such an event could have happened. In trying to give a meaning to Bryant's acts, numerous suggestions were put forward. One suggestion was that Bryant had been exposed to too many violent films or 'video nasties' which had influenced him to commit murder. Some media reports suggested that he had been bullied as a child because he was 'simple' or too effeminate-looking, and that the murders may have been an act of revenge upon the world for this cruelty. Still others commented that Bryant's father was violent and had beaten him when he was a child, and that this had led him into violence himself. Several calls for action were suggested. The major one was gun control, particularly in relation to semi-automatic weapons. New gun control regulations were seized upon as a strategy of risk containment. A secondary call for action was that violent films and videos be banned or censored. Further suggestion was made that individuals with a history of psychiatric illness be prevented from acquiring gun licences. All of these strategies were directed at regaining control over what was seen to be an unanticipated expression of evil, helping people deal with the horror, anger and frustration, the loss of control they felt in response to Martin Bryant's actions. These strategies are the products of late modern ways of thinking about, and reacting to, risk.

CHANGES IN THE MEANING OF RISK

Over the centuries, the word 'risk' has changed its meaning and its use has become far more common and applied to a plethora of situations. The word 'risk' appeared in German in references in the mid-sixteenth century and English in the second half of the seventeenth century. However, the Renaissance Latin term *riscum* had been in use long before in countries such as Germany (Luhmann 1993: 9). Most commentators link the emergence of the word and concept of risk with early maritime ventures in the pre-modern period, used to designate the perils that could compromise a voyage: 'At that time, risk designated the possibility of an objective danger, an act of God, a force majeure, a tempest or other peril of the sea that could not be imputed to wrongful conduct' (Ewald 1993: 226). This concept of risk, therefore, excluded the idea of human fault and responsibility. Risk was perceived to be a natural event such as a storm, flood or epidemic rather than a human-made one. As such, humans could do little but attempt to estimate roughly the likelihood of such events happening and take steps to reduce their impact.

Changes in the meanings and use of risk are associated with the emergence of modernity, beginning in the seventeenth century and gathering force in the eighteenth century. Modernity has been defined as 'the institutions and modes of behaviour established first of all in post-feudal Europe, but which in the twentieth century increasingly have become world-historical in their impact' (Giddens 1991: 14–15). Modernity is equivalent to the 'industrialized world', incorporating capitalism, the institutions of surveillance and nuclear weaponry as well as the process of industrialism. Modernity depends upon the notion emerging in the seventeenth-century Enlightenment that the key to human progress and social order is objective knowledge of the world through scientific exploration and rational thinking. It assumes that the social and natural worlds follow laws that may be measured, calculated and therefore predicted.

During the eighteenth and nineteenth centuries, the early modern European states sought to harness their populations productively and deal with the social changes and upheavals wrought by mass urbanization and industrialization as part of the Industrial Revolution. The science of probability and statistics was developed as a means of calculating the norm and identifying deviations from the norm, thus embodying the belief that rationalized counting and ordering would bring disorder under control (Hacking 1990). These fields were to become important to the modernist technical notion of risk. During the eighteenth century, the concept of risk had begun to be scientized, drawing upon new ideas in mathematics relating to probability. The development of statistical calculations of risk and the expansion of the insurance industry in the early modern era meant that the effects of phenomena that once were viewed as affecting individuals now could be calculated across populations. These phenomena could now be described, quantified and predicted and thus managed or avoided (Beck 1992a: 99). By the nineteenth century, the notion of risk was extended. It was no longer located exclusively in nature, but was 'also in human beings, in their conduct, in their liberty, in the relations between them, in the fact of their association, in society' (Ewald 1993: 226).

The modernist concept of risk represented a new way of viewing the world and its chaotic manifestations, its contingencies and uncertainties. It assumed that unanticipated outcomes may be the consequence of human action rather than the result of God's will, largely replacing earlier concepts of fate or *fortuna* (Giddens 1990: 30). Reddy claims that '[m]oderns had eliminated genuine indeterminacy, or "uncertainty", by inventing "risk". They had learnt to transform a radically indeterminate cosmos into a manageable one, through the myth of calculability' (1996: 237). Castel goes even further, arguing that the obsession with the prevention of risk in modernity is built upon

> a grandiose technocratic rationalizing dream of absolute
> control of the accidental, understood as the irruption of the
> unpredictable ... a vast hygienist Utopia plays on the
> alternate registers of fear and security, inducing a delirium
> of rationality, an absolute reign of calculative reason and a
> no less absolute prerogative of its agents, planners and
> technocrats, administrators of happiness for a life to which
> nothing happens.
>
> (Castel 1991: 289)

In modernity, risk, in its purely technical meaning, came to rely upon conditions in which the probability estimates of an event are able to be known or knowable. Uncertainty, in contrast, was used as an alternative term when these probabilities are inestimable or unknown. For example, in one form of economic theory developed in the mid-nineteenth century, risk was differentiated from uncertainty in this way. This distinction presupposed that there was a form of indeterminacy that was not subject to rational calculation of the likelihood of various alternative possibilities (Reddy 1996: 227). John Maynard Keynes, the influential English economic theorist, built on this distinction to argue that investors' behaviour should be classified as subject to uncertainty rather than the laws of risk because they were 'driven by "animal spirits"' which 'by their very nature were not subject to probabilistic or "risk" analysis' (cited in Reddy 1996: 229).

Modernist notions of risk also included the idea that risk could be both 'good' and 'bad'. The notion of risk as it developed in insurance is associated with notions of chance or probability, on one hand, and loss and damage, on the other. These two sets of notions come together in the concept of the accident, against which one insures oneself (Ewald 1991: 199). From this perspective, 'risk' is a neutral concept, denoting the probability of something happening, combined with the magnitude of associated losses or gains. In other words, there once was such a thing as a 'good' risk as well as a 'bad' risk (Douglas 1992: 23). This meaning of risk dominated until the beginning of the nineteenth century (Ewald 1991).

CONTEMPORARY CONCEPTS OF RISK

In the first decades of the twenty-first century, these fine distinctions between risk and uncertainty and 'good risk' and 'bad risk' have tended to be somewhat lost. The use of the word 'risk', as Douglas contends, now 'has not got much to do with probability calculations. The original connection is only indicated by arm-waving in the direction of possible science: the word *risk* now means danger; *high risk* means a lot of danger' (1992: 24, original emphases; see also Boholm 2012). Risk is now generally used to relate only to negative or undesirable outcomes, not positive outcomes. This is even often the case in more technical assessments of risk, where the potential benefits or positive aspects of risk tend to receive far less attention (Short 1984: 711). In the esoteric parlance of economic speculation, however, there remain such things as 'good risks' in relation to making a profit. It is recognized that risks must be taken to make money in speculative enterprises, and that often the greater the risk of losing one's money, the greater the return should things go well (Luhmann 1993: 71).

It is important to emphasize the 'always becoming' and transitory nature of risk. A risk is not a phenomenon that already exists; it is a phenomenon that may happen some time in the future, 'an unrealized potentiality' (Rigakos and Law 2009: 80). Further, risk is always a normative statement of morality because it incorporates the notion that it may involve harm to someone or something (ibid.: 80).

In everyday lay people's language, risk tends to be used to refer almost exclusively to a threat, hazard, danger or harm: we 'risk our life savings' by investing on the stock exchange, or 'put our marriage at risk' by having an affair. The term is also used more weakly to refer to a somewhat negative rather than disastrous outcome, as in the phrase 'If you go outside in this rain, you'll risk catching a cold.' In this usage, risk means somewhat less than a possible danger or a threat, more an unfortunate or annoying event. Risk is therefore a very loose term in everyday parlance. Issues of calculable probability are not necessarily important to the colloquial use of risk. Risk and uncertainty tend to be treated as conceptually the same thing: for example, the term 'risk' is often used to denote a phenomenon that has the potential to deliver substantial harm, whether or not the probability of this harm eventuating is estimable.

In contemporary Western societies, the noun 'risk' and the adjective 'risky' have become very commonly used in both popular and expert discourses. An apparatus of expert research, knowledge and advice has developed around the concept of risk: risk analysis, risk assessment, risk communication and risk management are all major fields of research and practice, used to measure and control risk in areas as far-ranging as medicine and public health, finance, the law, and business and industry. Indeed, the use of the term 'risk' appears to have been increasing in the past few decades. One study of the occurrence of 'risk' in academic journal article titles found an exponential growth between 1966 and 1982, particularly after the early 1970s (Inhaber and Norman 1982, cited in Short 1984: 712). A more specific search of some medical and epidemiological journals published in the United States, Britain and Scandinavia also found an increasing frequency of the use of the term over the years spanning 1967 and 1991, in which the late 1970s again marked the beginning of a period of rapid growth in the use of the term which accelerated in the late 1980s (Skolbekken 1995).

I undertook my own research to explore trends in the use of the term 'risk' in one Australian newspaper. I used the Factiva news media database to search for appearances of 'risk' in *The Australian* newspaper, a broadsheet which has a national focus. I looked at each year between 1997 and 2011 to see how many articles or headlines used 'risk' over that 15-year period. It is interesting to note that each year the number of uses of 'risk' gradually rose, reaching a peak in 2011. In 1997, 3,317 mentions of 'risk' appeared in the newspaper. Four years later, in 2001, this number had risen to 3,577, by 2006 to 5,280 and by 2011 'risk' was used 7,724 times in articles or headlines published in *The Australian*, more than double the incidence of its appearance in the first year in the period studied.

To investigate how the term was used in the newspaper articles, I selected the final month of the period examined, December 2011. During that month alone, 'risk' was used in many different ways and contexts: in relation to investments ('high risk and high potential', 'less risk for listed property trusts'), the economy ('the risk of inflation caused by losing control of the money supply'), the share-market and stock exchange ('share-markets went firmly "risk-off"'), managing the threat of protest or violence at the London Olympic Games (the torch relay was described as a 'manageable risk'), war (Australian troops 'risking their lives' in Afghanistan), the environment ('bushfire risk'), social security policy (teenage mothers needed to seek work or 'risk forfeiting their welfare payments'), political disputes ('breaking promises would risk rebellions in parliament'), health ('cancer risk of mobiles', 'at risk from the virus', 'the risk of asbestos'), politicians' orientation to risk management ('tendency to be risk averse') and their actions ('Obama's decision puts him at risk'), accidents (trains' 'risk of derailment'), illegal immigration (immigrants 'taking the risk' in making a perilous journey to Australia by sea and trying to enter illegally), threats to domestic or world economic security ('risks caused by an Asian market collapse'), world politics ('Tehran would risk alienating the few allies it has left'), global oil supply ('up to a fifth of the world's oil supply is at risk'), the provision of medical care in rural areas ('there is a real risk that services will be lost') and the loss of security in relation to computer systems ('at risk of having sensitive information published on other websites').

The proliferation of 'risk' as a term in reports in this particular newspaper both demonstrates the continuing currency of the term and the vast array of contexts in which it is employed. The overwhelming negative meaning of the term is also apparent from this identification of how risk is applied. The only report in which there was a positive meaning to risk was its use in relation to investments which may offer both 'high risk' and 'high potential'. Here high risk is positioned as a trade-off for higher financial gain. In every other case quoted above, risk represented a danger, threat or hazard which should be avoided if at all possible.

The news media frequently report on risks and play an important role not only in drawing audiences' attention to risks but in constructing what is considered a 'risk' and how it should be portrayed and managed. Reviews of how the news media tend to report risks (Anderson 2006; Hughes *et al.* 2006) have noted that they usually focus on phenomena that meet the definition of being 'newsworthy' and thus able to attract maximum audience attention. Catastrophic events that kill or injure many people at one time (as, for example, in a plane crash or natural disaster) receive far more attention than events unfolding over a long period of time. Unusual risks such as epidemics and famines tend to attract more media attention than those that are part of everyday life, such as car accidents. Risks that are bounded geographically also receive more media coverage than those that are dispersed, and risks that affect the region in which the audiences live are more likely to receive coverage than those further away. If particular individuals can be identified as the 'human angle' to give interest to the news story, then the risk with which they are associated will gain greater media attention, especially if they are celebrities. Accountability and blame feature prominently in news media reports of risks.

In the traditional news media certain kinds of experts are typically used to speak about and define what a 'risk' is, and these include people with medical or scientific authority, government officials and corporations. It is very difficult for those with alternative viewpoints to receive attention in news media coverage of risks (Anderson 2006; Hughes *et al.* 2006). Yet, since the advent of digital technologies linked to the internet, the traditional news media has begun to lose some of its authority, and along with this, lay people have greater opportunities to challenge expert views and perspectives. Ordinary citizens have been increasingly able to document what they view as risks via mobile digital devices and transmit them instantaneously to many others via the internet. Online discussion groups, activist websites and social media channels have provided a means for citizens to identify phenomena as risks and attempt to take action about them in what has been entitled 'e-activism' or 'internet activism' (Stoddart and MacDonald 2011; Tatarchevskiy 2011). These digital platforms also provide a forum for the exchange of expert information about risks, allowing lay people to evaluate and share this information. This use of digital media is particularly apparent in relation to health risks, in which manifold websites and apps for mobile digital devices are available for lay people to access information about risk factors for medical conditions, and many support groups exist for people who have been diagnosed with illnesses to exchange details about treatment options and experiences (Lupton 2012a).

The mass media and related websites and social media platforms have also been used as outlets for state-funded public health campaigns directed at persuading citizens to avoid health-related risks. Such campaigns have been directed at encouraging people to engage in safer sex, engage in moderate rather than excessive alcohol consumption, reduce their consumption of 'unhealthy' foods and beverages, engage in regular exercise, vaccinate their children, and give up smoking. Many such campaigns have adopted highly controversial, vivid, grotesque, fear-inducing and even frankly disgusting imagery to attempt to 'sell' their risk-reduction messages. Thus, for example, a New York City campaign directed at persuading residents to cut down on their consumption of sugary fizzy drinks because of their propensity to cause weight problems used a television commercial that showed a man drinking from a can. Instead of him swallowing a typical soda beverage, the advertisement showed the man enthusiastically chugging down pure, yellow-coloured and viscous fat. An Australian anti-tobacco television advertisement used the face of a woman with mouth cancer, her mouth eaten away by the disease, sores around her lips and several of her teeth missing, as she described how she has had to undergo chemotherapy and radiotherapy to treat this affliction caused by her smoking habit. Social marketing campaigns from several countries have used stark images of wobbly rolls of flesh on fat bodies in the attempt to publicize the dangers of obesity (these advertisements and those from other public health campaigns may be viewed at http://pinterest.com/dalupton/public-health-campaigns).

Many news and lifestyle media reports of risk, as well as citizen activist literature and social marketing campaigns, represent it as something to be avoided in the interests of preserving good health and well-being. On the other hand, some researchers have argued that the mass media and popular culture in general constantly glorify risk-taking activities such as sexual activity that may result in pregnancy or contracting a sexually transmissible disease, dangerous or reckless driving, excessive alcohol consumption or cigarette smoking and dangerous sporting activities. Such activities are often represented as glamorous, associated with wealth and beauty, normative concepts of femininity or masculinity or as being adventurous (Jette *et al.* 2007). This is particularly the case, for example, of television programmes such as *Jackass*, which depicts young men engaging in physical stunts, and computer games, advertisements and films that show reckless driving or violence (Fischer *et al.* 2011).

RISK ANXIETIES AND LATE MODERNITY

Various reasons have been suggested for the proliferation of the concept and language of risk in expert discourses over the past few decades. These include developments in probability statistics and computer technologies, allowing the statistical manipulation of large data sets in ways that were not previously possible, and the establishment of institutions and regulatory agencies to deal with such phenomena conceptualized as highly risky, such as nuclear energy. So too, changes in scientific thinking that have moved from paradigms of mono-causal determinism to those incorporating multiple causes and effects and an increasing value placed on scientific rationality as a basis for certainty have been suggested as focusing more attention on issues of risk (Short 1984; Douglas 1985; Skolbekken 1995). Some commentators have also pointed to changes in the nature of risks themselves as increasing expert and public concern. In the last part of the twentieth century, they argue, risks have become more globalized, less identifiable and more serious in their effects and therefore less easily manageable and anxiety-provoking (Beck 1992b).

At a deeper level of meaning, it may be argued that the contemporary obsession with the concept of risk has its roots in the changes inherent in the transformation of societies from pre-modern to modern and then to late modern (or postmodern, as some theorists prefer to describe the contemporary era). Late modernity or postmodernity generally refers to broader socio-economic and political changes that have taken place in Western societies since World War II, producing the sense for many people that we are 'living in new times' (Smart 1993: 15). These changes include the end of the Cold War, the breakdown of the socialist and communist states, the spread of communications technology and changes in familial relationships and the workplace wrought by the feminist movement, economic decline, and growing secularism. Most theorists agree that late modernity or postmodernity is characterized by a growing sense of the failed promises of early or 'simple' modernity and a tendency to challenge the key assumptions of this period, particularly those that unproblematically view science and medicine as the vanguards of progress. Thus, postmodernity has been defined as 'a more modest modernity, a sign of modernity having come to terms with its own limits and limitations' (ibid.: 12). Postmodernity, therefore, to a greater or lesser degree, is about a questioning of established thought, expression and practice, a deconstruction of tradition.

For many commentators, the late or postmodern era is characterized by uncertainty and ambivalence related to constant change and flux, cultural fragmentation and the breakdown of norms and traditions (see, for example, Giddens 1990; Massumi 1993; Lash and Urry 1994; Featherstone 1995). Time and space have become compressed, and there is an increasing rapid circulation of subjects and objects and an emptying-out of the established meaning of things and social relationships. Contemporary Western societies have been described as 'post-traditional' (Giddens 1994: 56), in that old traditions have been called into question, leaving greater uncertainty and insecurities.

All of these changes are seen as contributing to a particular way of understanding the self and the world that differs dramatically from earlier eras. For the individual, it is argued, these changes are associated with an intensifying sense of uncertainty, complexity, ambivalence and disorder, a growing distrust of social institutions and traditional authorities and an increasing awareness of the threats inherent in everyday life. Luhmann (1993: ix–xii) asserts that risk awareness is characterized by a fascination about extremely improbable circumstances with grave outcomes. This is not simply because the technological conditions exist for such circumstances to eventuate, because natural disasters have always occurred. The explanation for this fascination, he claims, is that today the decisions of individuals or organizations can be identified as the root cause of disasters, and therefore it can be demanded that their decisions be opposed so as to obviate danger. The concept of risk has gained importance in recent times because the dependence of society's future on decision-making has increased; it now is dominating ideas about the future.

For several writers on the late modern or postmodern era, the notion of risk is used as a keyword. It has come to stand as one of the focal points of feelings of fear, anxiety and uncertainty. Concern about risk has become intensified because of a general *fin-de-siècle* mood of malaise and disorientation, a sense that we are living in a time of endings and major disruptive social change. The term 'panic' has been used by some writers to describe the existential state of living in a postmodern society (Kroker and Kroker 1988). Massumi argues that individuals in late modernity experience a constant low-level fear, which is vague, not as sharp as panic or as localized as hysteria, but rather a 'kind of background radiation saturating existence' (1993: 24). He sees the assassination of American President John F. Kennedy in November 1963 as marking a divide in American culture: between the optimism of Enlightenment humanism and progress and the pessimism and uncertainty of the late modern era:

> Cracks began to open all around. There was no longer any safe ground. The shot could come from any direction, at any time, in any form ... Even pleasure no longer felt the same. Smoking was the insidious onset of a fatal ailment. Food becomes a foretaste of heart disease. The body itself was subversive of the 'self; in the 'youth culture', the very existence of the flesh was the onset of decline – Industrialization, once the harbinger of progress, threatened the world with environmental collapse ... Everywhere, imminent disaster.
>
> (Massumi 1993: 10)

Juxtaposed against this world of change are the meanings and strategies constructed around risk, which both spring from the uncertainties, anxieties and lack of predictability characteristic of late modernity and also attempt to pose solutions to them. Risk meanings and strategies are attempts to tame uncertainty, but often have the paradoxical effect of increasing anxiety about risk through the intensity of their focus and concern.

THE AIM OF THIS BOOK

Risk is a term that is understood and applied in different ways across the disciplinary fields of knowledge. In logic and mathematics, risk is a calculable problem, a function of probability and statistical measurements. The discipline of economics draws upon mathematical models, viewing risk as a resource that forms part of decision-making, a means of securing wealth or avoiding loss. Risk in economic terms is a phenomenon used to control the unknown by rendering it in terms of calculations and probabilities. In science and medicine, risk is an objective reality that can be measured, controlled and managed, again usually using mathematical models to measure and predict risk. For psychologists, risk is treated as a behavioural and cognitive phenomenon. Risk perception and responses are largely viewed as individual responses to a threat or hazard. In law, risk is a fault of conduct, an event that causes disorder and which involves costs and is therefore an object requiring legal intervention. From the perspective of linguistics, risk is a discursive term which has various meanings and communicative functions depending on how it is used, while philosophers occupy themselves with analysing the ontologies, epistemologies and ethical dimensions of risk (see Althaus 2005, for an elaboration of these varying perspectives, and Taylor-Gooby and Zinn 2006, for a comprehensive review of psychological and sociological approaches to risk).

Depending upon the discipline in which one places oneself, therefore, risk has a different ontological and epistemological status, and is researched and understood accordingly in different ways, using different tools, methods and frameworks of analysis. This book adopts a social and cultural perspective, drawing primarily upon sociological, anthropological, cultural geographical, and cultural studies approaches to risk. It analyses the ways in which people in Western societies give meaning to and deal with risk. A major premise of the book is that the identification of 'risks' takes place in the specific sociocultural, political and historical contexts in which we are located. To call something a 'risk' is to recognize its importance to our subjectivity and well-being. In some societies at some times, certain phenomena are selected as the focus for anxieties. In other societies and eras, other phenomena become prominent as 'risky'.

The point of this book is not to engage in discussion about the relative claims to truth of competing arguments about which phenomena should be considered 'real risks' or not, or how serious these risks are. Rather, it is to look at the ways in which the concept of risk operates in Western societies in the early decades of the twenty-first century, and its implications for how we think about ourselves, others, organizations, institutions and governments and the non-human world. Those phenomena that we single out and identify as 'risks' have an important ontological status in our understandings of selfhood and the social and material worlds. Societies – and within them, social institutions, social groups and individuals – need this selection process as part of their continued operation. Risk selection and the activities associated with the management of risk are central to ordering, function and individual and cultural identity.

At least seven major categories of 'risk' that currently appear to predominate in the concerns of individuals and institutions in Western societies can be identified. They are: (1) 'environmental risks', or those posed by pollution, radiation, chemicals, floods, fires, dangerous road conditions, and so on; (2) 'lifestyle risks', those believed to be related to food and drugs exercise habits, engagement in sexual activities, driving practices, stress and the like; (3) 'medical risks', those related to experiencing medical care or treatment (for example, drug therapy, surgery, childbirth, reproductive technologies, diagnostic tests); (4) 'interpersonal risks', related to intimate relationships, social interactions, love, sexuality, gender roles, friendship, marriage and parenting; (5) 'economic risks' implicated in unemployment or underemployment, borrowing money, investment, bankruptcy, destruction of property, failure of a business and so on; (6) 'criminal risks', those emerging from being a participant in or potential victim of illegal activities; and (7) 'political risks' such as political instability, terrorism, illegal immigration and citizen unrest.

That these categories of risk identified are prominent at this point in the history of Western societies is indicative of the nature of the broader sociocultural, political and economic context in which they acquire meaning. Our awareness and knowledge of these risks, and others, contribute to various aspects of subjectivity and social life, including how we live our everyday lives, how we distinguish our selves and the social groups of which we are members from other individuals and groups, how we perceive and experience our bodies, how we make decisions about relationships and families, how we spend our money, and where we choose to live, work and travel.

The term 'reflexivity' is often used in the sociological literature to denote the response of people in contemporary Western societies to risk, and this term appears throughout the book. Reflexivity means a response to conditions that arouse fear or anxiety that is active rather than passive. Reflexivity is a defining characteristic of all human action, involving the continual monitoring of action and its contexts (Giddens 1990: 36–7). It involves the weighing up and critical assessment of institutions and claim-makers, including those who speak with 'expert' voices about risk. As will be elaborated upon later in this book, some commentators argue that reflexivity is an inherent aspect of the contemporary meanings of risk: they are two sides of the same coin. The heightened sensitivity to risk evident in the late modern era is developed through a highly reflexive approach to the world.

'Discourse' is another term that often appears in the book, in my attempts to identify and speculate upon the sociocultural meanings and implications of risk. A discourse may be understood as a bounded body of knowledge and associated practices, a particular identifiable way of giving meaning to reality via words or imagery. Through discourses we perceive and understand the social, cultural and material worlds in which we move. Discourses both delimit and make possible what can be said and done about phenomena such as risk. There are a series of discourses on risk which may be identified that serve to organize the ways in which we perceive and deal with risk. Discourses are constantly in a state of flux: some come to prominence at certain times but then make way for others, and this has implications for our understanding of and response to phenomena. For example, the discourse on risk that represented it as both 'good' and 'bad' in early modernity has been superseded in late modernity by that which portrays it almost exclusively as 'bad'. Discourse analyses of risk reveal the shifting meanings around risk phenomena and the struggles over these meanings.

The prevalence of uncertainties and anxieties about what are seen to be risks, the nature of discourses on risk and how these influence the ways in which we conduct our selves and our social relationships and how societies are governed, are precisely the issues to which a number of major social and cultural risk theorists have recently directed their attention. The book draws on these theorists to examine and analyse the notion of risk as it is understood in contemporary Western societies. Chapter 2 discusses the major ways in which risk perception has been theorized in the social sciences, comparing the technico-scientific and cognitive psychological perspectives with sociocultural critiques, and particularly the social constructionist position on risk. Three major and distinctive theoretical perspectives in contemporary sociocultural theory – the 'cultural/symbolic', 'risk society' and 'governmentality' perspectives – are introduced in this chapter.

The next three chapters go on to discuss in detail these theoretical perspectives and the views of their major exponents on risk. Chapter 3 overviews the 'cultural/symbolic' perspective presented by anthropologist Mary Douglas and her followers, Chapter 4 discusses the writings of 'risk society' sociologists Ulrich Beck and Anthony Giddens, while Chapter 5 introduces the Foucauldian-influenced work of the 'governmentality' school. The final group of chapters organizes discussions of sociocultural theory around three important topics. Chapter 6 examines the notion of risk subjectivities, discussing the different ways in which people construct their understandings of risk and respond to risk. Chapter 7 looks at the more symbolic concept of Otherness, and its intertwined emotions of fear, disgust, fascination and desire, as they underlie notions of risk. The final chapter, Chapter 8, addresses the relatively neglected area of risk and pleasure, examining the ways in which people may deliberately engage in the transgressions of risk-taking in the attempt to escape the banalities of everyday life.

2

THEORIZING RISK

There are a number of ways in which the phenomenon of risk is addressed in the social scientific literature on risk perception. The most common is what some have referred to as the 'naïve realist' perspective, developed and expressed principally in technical and scientific approaches. One major approach adopting this perspective is that of cognitive science, based in psychology. An alternative perspective is social constructionism, advocated by those who are predominantly interested in the social and cultural aspects of risk. This chapter reviews these contrasting perspectives, discussing the epistemologies (knowledges) on which they are based and the different ways in which they represent risk, risk perception and the risk actor.

THE TECHNICO-SCIENTIFIC PERSPECTIVE

Technico-scientific approaches to risk, emerging from such fields as engineering, statistics, actuarialism, psychology, epidemiology and economics, bring together the notion of danger or hazard with calculations of probability. They define risk as 'the product of the probability and consequences (magnitude and severity) of an adverse event (i.e. a hazard)' (Bradbury 1989: 382). Various scientific instruments are employed to monitor, measure and calculate risks and to construct predictive models of how risks might affect individuals or populations. Debates over risk in these technico-scientific fields tend to revolve around issues of how well a risk has been identified or calculated, the level of seriousness of a risk in terms of its possible effects, how accurate is the 'science' that has been used to measure and calculate risk and how inclusive are the causal or predictive models that have been constructed to understand why risks occur and why people respond to them in certain ways. These approaches tend to be employed by those working within risk management, risk communication and risk analysis.

Much of the technico-scientific literature addresses what is seen to be the problem of conflict between scientific, industrial and government organizations and the public in relation to the health and environmental risks associated with science, technology and industry. The public is traditionally described as having become progressively concerned about such risks over the past half century or so and as directing a more critical and challenging eye upon the activities of industry and government. The literature on risk addressing this problem tends to attempt to identify the social and psychological factors influencing greater public cynicism and distrust of institutions and lay people's assessment of risk. The objective it seeks is to facilitate understanding between the public and institutions: 'to provide a route out of the ever-growing bitterness of clashes between affected publics and the managing institutions' (Brown 1989: 2).

One question that tends *not* to be asked in this research is 'How are risks constructed as social facts?', for the nature of risk is generally taken for granted. While most practitioners working in probabilistic risk assessment would acknowledge that 'subjectiveness' is an inevitable element of human judgement, and that therefore technical risk assessment is not value-free, the calculations they produce tend to be treated as if they were 'objective facts', or 'absolute truths' (Bradbury 1989: 382). Risks, according to this model, are pre-existing in nature and in principle are able to be identified through scientific measurement and calculation and controlled using this knowledge.

In the technico-scientific literature on risk there is sometimes evident an ill-masked contempt for lay people's lack of what is deemed to be 'appropriate' or 'correct' knowledge about risk. Lay people are often portrayed as responding 'unscientifically' to risk, using inferior and unsophisticated sources of knowledge such as 'intuition'. This is found, for example, in the Royal Society's (1992) report on risk, which drew a distinction between 'objective' and 'subjective' risk. It was argued in this report that a range of 'objective' risks exist in any situation, to which individuals and social groups respond in more or less 'subjective' ways.

COGNITIVE PSYCHOLOGY

Exponents of the cognitive psychological approach are primarily interested in using various psychological models of human behaviour to identify the ways in which people respond cognitively and behaviourally to risk at an individual level. In this literature, 'the hazard is taken as the independent variable and people's response to it as dependent' (Douglas 1985: 25). The 'objective facts' of risk as they are calculated by 'experts' are contrasted with the subjective understandings of lay people, which are seen as being more or less accurate compared with these 'facts'. Such risk calculations tend not to acknowledge the role played by the 'ways of seeing' on the part of the experts themselves that produce such calculations. Their understandings of risk are represented as neutral and unbiased. As such, many of these approaches tend to take a technico-scientific perspective.

Some psychologists take a psychometric perspective, attempting to measure the relative influence of different cognitive factors in shaping lay response. The psychometric approach has been the most influential model in risk analysis research (Siegrist *et al.* 2005). Psychometric researchers focus on the 'mental strategies' or 'heuristics' used in making judgements about risk and which are viewed as often leading to 'large and persistent biases' on the part of lay people (Slovic 1987: 281). To do so they use psychological testing to quantify mental processes when people are assessing risk, constructing a 'cognitive map' of these processes in the attempt to understand how people respond differently to risk (Siegrist *et al.* 2005). Respondents are typically asked to complete questionnaires and their responses are converted into values on scales which demonstrate what their responses are compared with other people who have completed the questionnaire. Various dimensions of the risks involved, as identified by the researchers, are singled out and measured independently of each other to see how the respondents assess them. Respondents may also be measured for certain personality attributes, such as sensation-seeking, curiosity, desire for excitement, neuroticism or extroversion and their risk assessments measured against others (Llewellyn 2008).

Several psychometric researchers have developed a 'taxonomy' by which hazards are categorized and dealt with cognitively. They have argued that lay people overestimate and underestimate some categories of risk, and find it difficult to assess risk using probabilities. For instance, it has been found by psychometric researchers that lay people are more likely to calculate that risk is likely to occur if information related to it is available and easily recalled, and tend to overestimate risk related to circumstances where it can be easily imagined as happening to oneself. It has also been found that people are more likely to be concerned about risks that they see as being close to them. Risks that are seen to be rare but memorable tend to be overestimated while those that are considered to be common and less serious are underestimated. Risks that are perceived as familiar or voluntary are considered more acceptable and less likely to happen than those that are perceived to be new or imposed. People tend to be risk averse when faced with gains and risk seeking when faced with losses. Psychometric researchers have also reported that disasters that receive a high level of media attention arouse more concern than those that do not, even if they are relatively rare occurrences; dangers which are seen to occur in a cluster are considered more serious than an equivalent number of events that happen over a longer period of time; and the consequences of catastrophes that occur immediately arouse more concern than those that are delayed (see Slovic 1987; Siegrist *et al.*

2005; Taylor-Gooby and Zinn 2006; and Llewellyn 2008, for overviews of psychometric research).

An epistemological uncertainty is evident in relation to the concept of risk as it is used by psychometric and other psychological research endeavours, even though this does not tend to be openly acknowledged by its exponents. The research tends to provide 'a subjectivist interpretation within a realist paradigm' (Bradbury 1989: 384). Some psychometric researchers argue that 'actual risks' do exist but they can only ever be interpreted as perceptions. Others continue to argue that some definitions of risk (particularly those made by 'experts') are 'real' and 'correct'. Some, confusingly, include both concepts of risk in their work interchangeably (ibid.: 384).

Psychometric risk analyses and other cognitive science approaches are founded on a theory of rational behaviour and the notion of the ideal rational investigator and the rational, risk-perceiving agent. They represent the individual as an information-processing unit, taking in information about risk and dealing with it in certain ways that are typically represented as biased or limited. The cognitive science approach, therefore, often constructs individuals as calculating and emotion-free actors, assuming that they all share the responses and preferences of the actor in utilitarian philosophy:

> Warm-blooded, passionate, inherently social beings though we think we are, humans are presented in this context as hedonic calculators calmly seeking to pursue private interests. We are said to be risk-aversive, but, alas, so inefficient in handling information that we are unintentional risk-takers; basically we are fools.
>
> (Douglas 1992: 13)

Douglas further asserts that cognitive science presents too narrow a view of rational action, so that anything outside this becomes viewed as irrational: 'So instead of a sociological, cultural, and ethical theory of human judgement, there is an unintended emphasis on perceptual pathology' (1985: 3).

Another difficulty with such approaches is that they tend to reduce the meanings and behaviours associated with risk perception and assessment to the individualistic level. Cognitive science does not generally take into account the symbolic meanings, created through the social world, which humans give to things and events. Perception is limited to how humans see and understand the world through their senses and brain functioning, without acknowledging the ways in which cultural conceptual categories mediate judgement. People tend to be positioned outside the cultural and political frameworks, relationships and institutions within which they construct their beliefs and engage in behaviours. In such research, individuals are therefore represented as atomized and self-interested, ideally behaving in response to their carefully considered calculations of risk as it affects them individually. They are portrayed as free actors who are constrained only by their ignorance about the threat to which they may be exposed or their lack of self-efficacy in feeling able to do something about a risk.

In their focus on measurable personality attributes and beliefs that can be easily quantified, such models tend to take a rigid, uni-dimensional perspective on human behaviour. Risks and behaviours that are associated with such risks are themselves singled out for attention in this literature as often separate from other risks and behaviours. This is convenient for psychometric statistical testing and modelling, but reduces and over-simplifies such phenomena. An individual is categorized, for example, as either a sensation-seeker or someone who would rather avoid thrills. The possibility that people may oscillate between the two based on the context in which they find themselves is not allowed for in these models.

The recent development and use of what is termed 'affect heuristics' in the cognitive psychology literature have been lauded as one of risk analysis researchers' most important accomplishments in the past three decades (Greenberg *et al.* 2012). The concept of the affect heuristic focuses on the role played by emotion in influencing individuals' responses to risk. Here again, however, the role of emotion tends to be positioned in linear models of individuals' thought processes as part of their responses to and identification of risks. In 'appraisal' models of behaviour, individuals' emotional responses to risks – their 'appraisals' – are identified as part of their reactions to risks. It is argued that cognitive appraisals relating to such factors as control, fairness, importance and certainty precede emotional responses, which in turn shape the acceptance or rejection of risks (see, for example, Dohle *et al.* 2012). A different psychological model, the 'risk information seeking and processing model' positions emotions as 'indirect predictors of risk information seeking' (Catellier and Yang 2012). Here emotions are viewed as diverting people's ability to rationally or cognitively assess risks, influencing irrational behaviour. A linear model is proposed in which emotion leads to the development of a judgement or a choice which then leads to a particular risk assessment. There is little room here for recognizing that people may feel ambivalent about risks, that they may move back and forth in their emotional responses and judgements about risk, and that indeed emotional responses, rather than being separate from and 'interfering' in rational decision-making, are inextricably intertwined with risk judgements or rationalities.

It would appear that at least some researchers using cognitive and social psychological approaches to risk perception have begun to incorporate social and cultural processes into their models of individual behaviour as part of a matrix of influences which are viewed as influencing risk responses. Since the late 1980s some sociocultural perspectives on risk – particularly those offered by Mary Douglas – have been taken up enthusiastically by some researchers in cognitive science and other technico-scientific fields interested in risk perception and risk management. This usage, however, has been somewhat selective and has, at times, somewhat distorted Douglas' views (see the discussion in Chapter 3 following a detailed review of Douglas' writings).

As part of adopting Douglas' work, the psychological literature on risk has begun to refer to 'worldviews', or belief systems on how the world operates that are developed through membership of social groups as well as through personal experience. In particular, the 'social amplification of risk' model, a social psychology approach, has become more dominant in the risk assessment and risk communication literature in recent years. This model encompasses the idea that risks which are considered relatively minor by experts are viewed as more serious (or indeed 'exaggerated') by the public because of social and cultural as well as psychological factors (or vice versa). It is contended that 'risk signals' are amplified, or rendered larger and more important, or else attenuated, or rendered less important, via social processes that 'transfer' these signals in a 'distorted' way (Masuda and Garvin 2006; Busby and Duckett 2012). The aim of such research is to understand why some phenomena are treated by lay people as more or less serious than is pronounced by expert judgements (Jackson 2006).

As is evident from the type of language used in describing this model, it adopts a stimulus-message-response perspective on the ways in which information about risks is conveyed to the public, and views what exponents of the model describe as 'social processes' as interferences in the correct transmission of risk information. These social processes include the mediation of risks via the mass media, social institutions and organizations such as government agencies or social networks and groups such as activist groups. Those individuals or social groups who are identified as 'risk amplifiers' are positioned as wrongly exaggerating the risks of a phenomenon which has been judged by expert assessors to be benign, while those who are viewed as 'risk attenuators' are playing down the importance of risks as determined by expert judgement. What the exponents define as 'social' or 'cultural' becomes viewed in a similar way to emotion in the models described above: as 'super variables' or influences – indeed 'interferences' or 'biases' – in the development of lay risk perception which detract from rational decision-making. There is still regular reference to non-experts relying on emotional judgements rather than 'facts' and 'contextual biasing forces' as distorting lay judgements compared with expert judgements of risk (see, for example, Fleming *et al.* 2012; Greenberg *et al.* 2012).

SOCIOCULTURAL PERSPECTIVES

Sociocultural perspectives on risk emphasize the very aspects that cognitive psychological and other technico-scientific approaches have been criticized for neglecting: the social and cultural contexts in which risk is understood, lived, embodied and negotiated. They have emerged from such disciplines as cultural anthropology, philosophy, sociology, social history, cultural and media studies, gender studies, critical social psychology, cultural geography and science and technology studies. The boundaries between these disciplines and sub-disciplines have tended to blur somewhat over the past few decades. As a result, scholars within these areas often use similar theoretical perspectives, and this is evident in the literature on the sociocultural aspects of risk.

As I noted in Chapter 1, theorists on the sociocultural dimensions on risk could loosely be categorized into at least three major groups based on the perspective adopted. The perspective advanced by anthropologist Mary Douglas and her colleagues and followers constitutes the 'cultural/symbolic' perspective. A second group is that of the 'risk society' theorists, dominated by the sociologists Ulrich Beck and Anthony Giddens. A third group may be described as the 'governmentality' theorists, who draw on the writings of the French philosopher Michel Foucault.

Those scholars adopting the 'cultural/symbolic' perspective direct their attention to the ways in which notions of risk are used to establish and maintain conceptual boundaries between self and Other, with a particular interest in how the human body is used symbolically and metaphorically in discourses and practices around risk. The sociologists adopting the 'risk society' perspective are predominantly interested in the macro-social processes they see as characteristic of late modern societies and their relation to concepts of risk. These processes include reflexive modernization, or the move towards criticism of the outcomes of modernity, and individualization, or the breaking down of traditional norms and values. 'Governmentality' scholars have taken up in particular Foucault's insights on governmentality and on ethical self-formation to explore risk in the context of surveillance, discipline and regulation of populations, and how concepts of risk construct particular norms of behaviour which are used to encourage individuals to engage voluntarily in self-regulation in response to these norms.

While, as will be explained in detail in later chapters, there are some major differences between these perspectives, their exponents all tend to argue that there are a number of important new features in notions of risk in contemporary Western societies. They see risk as having become a central cultural and political concept by which individuals, social groups and institutions are organized, monitored and regulated. The following insights are central to all three major perspectives: (1) risk has become an increasingly pervasive concept of human existence in Western societies; (2) risk is a central aspect of human subjectivity; (3) risk is seen as something that can be managed through human intervention; and (4) risk is associated with notions of choice, responsibility and blame.

There is another loose typology that can be used to characterize the more discrete epistemological and methodological positions taken up within sociocultural investigations into risk. This typology distinguishes between structuralist, poststructuralist, biophilosophical, phenomenologist and psychoanalytic approaches.

Structuralists approach their analyses of risk primarily by seeking to identify the ways in which underlying cultural structures, hierarchies and categories serve to define risk knowledges and practices. They may adopt a functional structuralist approach, interested in how social and cultural structures and systems serve to maintain social order and the status quo and deal with 'deviance', or divergence from accepted norms and social rules concerning behaviour. Mary Douglas and some of her followers may be categorized as functional structuralists (see Chapter 3). Alternatively, a critical structuralist approach may be taken, which builds on the Marxist critical legacy to focus more on social conflict, inequities and dissent and the need for social change in relation to risk. Critical structuralists tend to be interested in critiquing the ways in which social institutions (such as government, the economic system and the legal system) wield power over individuals, reducing their capacity for agency and autonomy. The work of Ulrich Beck and Anthony Giddens (discussed in Chapter 4) mainly uses a critical structuralist approach.

The poststructuralist perspective, as it has been adopted to explore issues of risk, builds largely upon Foucauldian theory (Chapter 5). Given its reliance upon the work of Foucault, the 'governmentality' position on risk can be described as poststructuralist. Poststructuralism emphasizes the importance of identifying the discourses that participate in the construction of notions of realities, meanings and understandings. Exponents of poststructuralism tend to focus less on what they see to be the overly rigid definitions of structures identified in structuralism. They are more interested in change and flux in social structures and meanings. There is also a different view on power relations in poststructuralist writings than is generally put forward in structuralist accounts. A central preoccupation of poststructuralists is with the relationship between power and knowledge. They point out that power relations are always implicated with knowledge and that no knowledge, therefore, can be said to be 'neutral' or 'disinterested' (including poststructuralists' own truth claims). Individuals are seen not to be fixed in social or cultural identities, but constantly shifting, the products of various combinations of power–knowledge formations. It is viewed as operating through manifold sites, rather than predominantly through monolithic social institutions. Power is seen as not simply coercive or oppressive, as critical structuralism tends to have it, but also as productive and inevitably present in any social relation.

The term 'biophilosophical' is used to describe a range of philosophical approaches directed at understanding the contingencies and dynamic nature of bodies (van Loon 2002). This term encompasses the writings of the French philosophers Deleuze and Guattari as well as writers in science and technology studies such as Haraway and Latour. This perspective also overlaps to a significant degree with Foucauldian and other poststructuralist analyses. These theorists have been used by some researchers to conceptualize risks as virtual, fragile and multiple phenomena which are dispersed among networks. The notion of 'assemblages', or constantly changing configurations of human bodies, discourses, practices, ideas, non-human bodies and material objects, is central to this perspective. These approaches to risk highlight the importance of space, place and material objects in configuring risk concepts, technologies and practices. They also emphasize the ways in which risks are actively made – brought into being as 'risk assemblages' – by a gathering of various agents and actors.

Phenomenological or hermeneutic accounts of risk are interested in the situated meanings that are given to risk. Exponents of this perspective, therefore, are less interested in the macrostructures organizing and constraining the meanings of risk than are the structuralists. Rather, they turn their attention towards 'lived experience', or how individuals experience their world as an interpretive reality with the use of shared commonsense meanings and knowledges. Phenomenologists argue that the meanings of risk differ from locale to locale: that is, in the micro-context of risk meanings. Phenomenological accounts examine how specific actors (or sub-groups) within a certain sociocultural setting construct their risk understandings as part of their interactions with others, albeit within the broader frame of social structures. Meaning is not simply drawn from the social environment, therefore: it also works the other way, with social actors influencing their environments. Chapters 6 and 8 draw upon phenomenological investigations in addressing issues of risk and subjectivity and the pleasurable aspects of risk-taking.

The psychoanalytic theoretical perspective is interested in exploring the unconscious psychodynamic processes which mediate people's responses to other people and to objects and events. In relation to ideas about risk it is perhaps best represented in the work of Julia Kristeva and Elizabeth

Grosz, both feminist psychoanalytic theorists who have built upon and extended Mary Douglas' theories. While Kristeva and Grosz do not explicitly discuss the topic of risk, many of their observations on the notion of the 'abject' have strong relevance for an understanding of the ways in which notions of risk are linked to those of the body and Otherness. The abject is that which both disgusts or horrifies and fascinates us, which we seek to expel from our bodies and our selves as part of maintaining our sense of autonomy and individuation. As such, the abject is fraught with symbolic riskiness, in the sense of challenging our sense of subjectivity and individuality, our ability to demarcate ourselves from others, our feelings of purity and containment (see Chapter 7 for further elaboration of this concept in relation to risk).

SOCIAL CONSTRUCTIONIST POSITIONS

In the sociocultural literature there are a range of positions on risk that are taken up, with some falling more towards a relativist and others more towards a realist approach, and yet others somewhere in the middle. Sometimes risk is talked about as if it were based on objective facts about dangers and hazards, amenable to rationalistic calculation, which are then mediated, perceived and responded to in particular ways via social, cultural and political processes. This may be described as the 'weak' social constructionist thesis. This position overlaps to some extent with those cognitive psychological studies (some of which are discussed above) which go beyond a focus on individuals to directing attention at social group membership. The 'weak' social constructionist position has also been described by some as 'critical realism'.

The critical realist approach contends that the real social and natural world exists apart from and thus is independent of human perception and understanding. Human knowledge of reality is fallible and incomplete and is historically, socially, culturally and politically situated. In relation to risk, the critical realist position both acknowledges that phenomena exist that may harm people's health or well-being in some way (whether these are psychological, physical, emotional or financial) and that these phenomena are singled out and labelled as 'risks' (or not, as the case may be) via social and cultural processes and assumptions. Critical realists argue that more and more phenomena are identified and named as 'risks' (hence the increasing use of the term in newspaper articles as time progresses, as described in Chapter 1). Where once cigarette smoking, high cholesterol levels or driving without a seatbelt were not considered 'risks' to human health, now they are labelled and treated as such. These phenomena existed prior to their labelling as 'risks' and had real effects on health status but the ways in which they are viewed, managed and regulated have changed since their identification as 'risks'.

Critical realism argues that the phenomena that are labelled 'risks' exist whether or not we apprehend them, as do those potentially harmful phenomena that we choose not to call 'risks'. Individuals can only ever achieve a partial understanding of the real world and knowledges are always, therefore, subject to critique, revision and change. This perspective rejects a strong constructionist approach, seeing this as undermining efforts to 'do something' about phenomena which may have harmful effects on people or the environment. It has been positioned as a third way between naïve realist approaches and extreme constructionist perspectives (Houston 2001; Tulloch 2008a; Rigakos and Law 2009).

Exponents of the more relativist perspective, or the 'strong' social constructionist position, contend, as Ewald has put it, that: 'Nothing is a risk in itself; there is no risk in reality. But on the other hand, anything *can* be a risk; it all depends on how one analyses the danger, considers the event' (1991: 199, original emphasis). As I will go on to demonstrate in later chapters, the 'risk society' and 'cultural/symbolic' approaches tend to adopt a critical realist approach while exponents of the 'governmentality' approach generally take a strong relativist position.

Those who have adopted social constructionism, regardless of the strength of their position, tend to argue that a risk is never fully objective or knowable outside of belief systems and moral positions: what we measure, identify and manage as risks are always constituted via pre-existing knowledges and discourses. This approach to risk is indebted to writings in the sociology of knowledge, the sociology of science and technology and theorizing from poststructuralist and postmodernist perspectives. Social constructionists argue that humans and their social world exist in a dialectical relationship, in which each creates the other. Although the material and social worlds are experienced by most individuals as objective, pre-existing realities, these realities involve the reproduction of meaning and knowledges through social interaction and socialization and rely upon shared definitions. Because of the continually constructed nature of reality, its meanings are precarious and subject to change.

From the constructionist perspective, all knowledge about risk is bound to the sociocultural contexts in which this knowledge is generated, whether in relation to scientists' and other experts' knowledges or lay people's knowledges. Scientific knowledge, or any other knowledge, is never value-free but rather is always the product of a way of seeing. A risk, therefore, is not a static, objective phenomenon, but is constantly constructed and negotiated as part of the network of social interaction and the formation of meaning. 'Expert' judgements of risk, rather than being the 'objective' and 'neutral' and therefore 'unbiased' assessments as they tend to be portrayed in the technico-scientific literature, are regarded as being equally as constructed through implicit social and cultural processes as are lay people's judgements.

For social constructionists, it is not a matter of doing more research to obtain a clearer view of exactly to which risks people are exposed. Instead, the primary focus is on examining how concepts of risk are part of lived experiences, logics and perspectives. There is a cultural pattern in the ways in which certain phenomena are identified and dealt with as 'risks' and this pattern is subject to change over time and space. Rather than seeing 'risks' as realities lying outside of society and culture, therefore, they can be viewed as conglomerations of meanings, logics and beliefs cohering around material phenomena, giving these phenomena form and substance. We can only ever know and experience risks through our specific location in a particular sociocultural context. This approach to risk highlights the importance of understanding the embeddedness of understandings and perceptions of risk, and emphasizes that these understandings and perceptions often differ between actors who are located in different contexts and thus bring competing logics to bear upon risk.

Debates about risk always involve questions of cultural representation and meaning and political positions. As I observed above, the weak social constructionist position sees risks as cultural mediations of 'real' dangers and hazards. For the strong social constructionist position, by contrast, a 'hazard' or 'danger' itself is also seen as socially constructed, coming into social existence when human actors recognize and label it as such (Fox 1999, 2002, 2011). Judgements about risk, therefore, are not simply cultural interpretations of objective dangers or hazards. What is deemed a 'danger' or 'hazard' in one historical or cultural context may not be so identified in another, and this has implications for how knowledges and understandings about risks are developed. Thus, hazards and dangers are not viewed as preceding concepts of risk, but themselves as brought into being through judgements of risk. Risk judgements are themselves constructed through prior knowledge and experience of the world, based on personal embodied experiences, observations and emotional responses, discussions with others and access to expert knowledges. Objects, practices, spaces, places, individuals, and so on are configured as 'dangerous' or 'hazardous' through the application of risk assessments to these phenomena.

The strong social constructionist approach also insists that once a risk, danger or hazard is brought into being, this is by no means the end of the process. Risks are mutable, contingent upon further acts, framings and practices, they are unstable. A risk that once was seen to exist disappears, or becomes less clamouring for attention, but then may re-emerge. What is of importance for a sociocultural analysis of risk is the ways in which certain linkages are defined. The task of constructing a risk object is essentially a rhetorical process, performed in specialized texts or in public arenas, and usually involves building networks of heterogeneous risk objects. It often involves intense struggles over meaning, particularly in relation to those actors who are deemed to be responsible for the risk object. These struggles are complemented by struggles with a variety of human and non-human actors to identify and control risk objects (Hilgartner 1992).

'Expert' knowledges – particularly those emerging from science, medicine, the 'psy' disciplines (psychology, psychiatry, counselling), social work, the law and economics – embedded within organizational contexts and often mediated through the mass media, are central to the construction and publicizing of risk. Debates among scientists and other experts often occur around such uncertainties as what is considered adequate 'proof' that a phenomenon is hazardous, how acceptable the level of hazard is, and what the consequences of attempting to control that hazard might be. While disputes over the validity of technical data may contribute to these debates, at a more fundamental level, different systems of values and ways of seeing shape experts' judgements of these data. Experts, in seeking validity for their knowledge claims, do not tend to acknowledge the situated and localized nature of their risk calculations and prognoses, however, preferring to represent them as objective universal truths. Neither do they acknowledge that their knowledges are culturally shaped, evincing particular assumptions about the 'natural', the 'cultural' and what it means to be human (Wynne 1996).

Over the past three decades, we have seen HIV/AIDS and 'mad cow disease' (bovine spongiform encephalopathy) emerge as new health risks and then recede in prominence; the SARS virus and the swine and avian flu pandemics have been discovered, attracted a high level of attention and then largely dropped from public view; and the world has been regarded as threatened by an 'obesity epidemic', which remains as a current preoccupation for health authorities, the mass media and governments. In all these cases, bodily symptoms and signs were interpreted in certain ways by influential actors and networks – scientists, medical researchers and practitioners, epidemiologists, public health officials, centres for disease control, public health notification systems – brought together and named as a syndrome or medical condition. The knowledges accumulated by these expert actors, networks and practices interacted with embodied experiences, non-expert forms of knowledges, mass media representations and spaces to construct the 'reality' of the particular health risk.

These actors and knowledges may struggle to define this 'reality': they may contest and challenge each other as well as work together. Thus, for example, there is currently a lively debate in the social science literature concerning the 'reality' of the obesity epidemic which has been positioned as a major health risk for populations around the globe. Critics of 'obesity discourse' contend that medical and public health researchers and officials have misinterpreted data on obesity in their argument that exceeding a certain body mass is a major risk to an individual's health and longevity. These writers argue that the research supporting the notion of the 'obesity epidemic' and linking fatness to ill health is far from conclusive. They draw attention to the common conflation of the terms 'overweight' and 'obesity' and the inaccuracy of the commonly used measure of body weight, the body mass index (BMI), and challenge the causal relationship between fatness and the diseases which are commonly attributed to it (see, for example, Gard and Wright 2005; Gard 2011; Rich *et al.* 2011).

If a 'risk' is understood as a product of perception and cultural understanding, then to draw a distinction between 'real' risks (as measured and identified by 'experts') and 'false' risks (as perceived by members of the public) is irrelevant. Both perspectives are describing forms of risk, and both lead to certain actions. It is the ways in which these understandings are constructed and acted upon that is considered important, not the extent to which one perspective may be considered to be more 'accurate' or less 'biased' than the other, for this distinction is also considered to be irrelevant. The questions that might be asked about risk from the constructionist perspective, therefore, are very different from those asked from the technico-scientific perspective. They include the following (adapted from Hall 1997: 45–6): What statements are used to construct certain kinds of knowledges about risk at a particular historical moment and sociocultural setting? What rules prescribe certain ways of talking about risk and exclude other ways? What types of subjects and assemblages are constructed through risk discourses? How does knowledge about risk acquire authority, a sense of embodying the 'truth' about it? What practices are used in institutions and by individuals for dealing with the subjects of risk discourses? And, How do new discourses on risk emerge, supplanting other discourses, and what are the effects of this for risk knowledges and risk assemblages?

CONCLUDING COMMENTS

This chapter has provided a review of various epistemological and methodological approaches used to analyse the role of risk in subjectivity and social relations. Table 2.1 provides a model of how these different approaches may be mapped against each other, based on the notion of a continuum that moves from the naïve realist position at one pole to 'strong' social constructionist, or relativist, positions on risk, at the other pole. Any such schema will inevitably be somewhat reductive – some approaches to risk, for example, may

Table 2.1 Epistemological approaches to risk in the social sciences

Epistemological position	Associated perspectives and theories	Key questions
Naïve realism: Risk is an objective hazard, threat or danger that exists and can be measured independently of social and cultural processes. Risk perceptions may be distorted or biased through social and cultural frameworks of interpretation.	Technico-scientific perspective.	What risks exist? How should we measure and manage them? How should information about risks be effectively communicated to the public? How to reduce 'bias' in the public's responses?
	Cognitive psychology.	How do people respond cognitively to risks? What worldviews shape their responses?

Table 2.1 Continued

Epistemological position	Associated perspectives and theories	Key questions
'Weak' constructionist/ critical realism: Risk is an objective hazard, threat or danger that is inevitably mediated through social and cultural processes and can never be known in isolation from these processes.	'Risk society' perspective. 'Cultural symbolic' perspective.	What is the relationship of risk to the structures and processes of late modernity? How is risk understood in different sociocultural contexts? Why are some dangers named as 'risks' and other not? How does risk operate as a symbolic boundary measure? What are the situated contexts of risk?
'Strong' constructionist: Nothing is a risk in itself – what we understand to be a 'risk' (or hazard, threat or danger) is the product of historically, socially and culturally contingent 'ways of seeing'.	'Governmentality' perspective. Poststructuralism. Biophilosophy.	How do the discourses and practices around risk operate in the construction of subjectivity, embodiment and social relations? How does risk operate as part of governmental strategies and rationalities? How are risk assemblages configured?

Source: author

combine aspects of more than one perspective rather than being able to be neatly slotted into a specific category. Nonetheless, the model is useful as a device in demonstrating the links between the epistemological position and associated perspectives and theories that have been discussed in this chapter, as well as outlining the key questions about risk that are asked from the various approaches. Later chapters build upon this foundational discussion in providing greater detail about various approaches to risk in sociocultural theorizing and research.

3

RISK AND CULTURE

The cultural anthropologist Mary Douglas has been a pivotal figure in sociocultural analyses of risk, and she is the primary exponent of and influence in 'cultural/symbolic' perspectives on risk. Douglas' approach to risk is best understood as part of a trajectory of theorizing on the body, selfhood and the regulation of contamination and danger that she began 50 years ago, in which the symbolic aspects of judgements about danger, pollution and Otherness were identified. Risk, for Douglas, is a contemporary Western strategy for dealing with danger and Otherness. Much of her writings on risk seek to explain why it is that some dangers are identified as 'risks' and others are not. Her main explanations revolve around the importance for social groups, organizations or societies to maintain the boundaries between self and Other, deal with social deviance and achieve social order. As such, her approach and those of her followers may be described as taking a functional structuralist approach to risk.

This chapter reviews the most integral aspects of Douglas' work on risk. It begins with a discussion of the importance of culture in constructions of risk, moves onto issues concerning purity, danger and the body and then looks at the relationship between risk and blame. The chapter concludes with discussion of the concept of grid-group as it structures cultural responses to risk.

THE IMPORTANCE OF CULTURE

In her extensive writings on risk, Douglas is trenchant in her critique of cognitive psychological and other technico-scientific approaches to understanding risk. She is particularly critical of the individualistic approach taken by the psychological researchers dominating risk perception research in their focus on processes of cognition and choice. Douglas contends that '[t]he professional discussion of cognition and choice has no sustained theorizing about the social influences which select particular risks for attention. Yet it is hard to maintain seriously that perception of risk is private' (1985: 3). The difference that is commonly observed between 'expert' and 'lay' judgements of risk is founded not in the fact that lay people cannot think in terms of probabilities, as some psychometric risk analysts have contended (see Chapter 2), but rather that other concerns are brought to bear in the ways they judge risk. These concerns are essentially cultural rather than individual: 'individuals do not try to make independent choices, especially about big political issues. When faced with estimating probability and credibility, they come already primed with culturally learned assumptions and weightings' (Douglas 1992: 58).

So too, in discussing why people may prefer to engage in activities they know to be labelled as 'risky', Douglas argues that '[a] refusal to take sound hygienic advice is not to be attributed to weakness of understanding. It is a preference. To account for preferences there is only cultural theory' (1992: 103). Lay responses to risk should not be considered as erroneous or biased if they differ from expert assessments. Rather, their use and value within a particular cultural context need to be acknowledged. Douglas further argues that the heuristics or mental models that people use to make judgements about risks should not be considered merely as 'cognitive aids for the individual decision-maker' (1985: 80), as the psychometric perspective would have it. Instead, they should be regarded as shared conventions, expectations and cultural categories that are founded on clear social functions and responsibilities. She describes culture as a 'mnemonic system' (ibid.: 81) which helps people to calculate risks and their consequences. Not only does culture help people understand risk, it also contributes to a communal rather than an individualistic notion of risk, taking into account mutual obligations and expectations:

> A community uses its shared, accumulated experience to determine which foreseeable losses are most probable, which probable losses will be most harmful, and which harms may be preventable. A community also sets up the actors' model of the world and its scale of values by which different consequences are reckoned grave or trivial.
>
> (Douglas 1985: 69)

Douglas emphasizes the cultural relativity of judgements about risks, including the differences between groups within the same culture in terms of what is considered a risk and how acceptable it is thought to be. Traditional risk research ignores the conceptual, ethical and moral difficulties around the definition of equality and justice – 'each type of society has its custom-built ethical system' (Douglas 1985: 15) – and thus fails to acknowledge or address the related problem of how risk is to be judged acceptable or not. It is pointless, therefore, to concentrate on providing 'better' communication or more education about risk to the lay public as a means of settling risk disputes, for the issue is not one of misguided perception but rather is the result of clashes in political, moral and aesthetic judgements on risk.

As is evident from the title of her most recent collection of essays on risk, *Risk and Blame: Essays in Cultural Theory* (1992), Douglas' approach to risk strongly emphasizes the political use of the concept of risk in attributing blame for danger threatening a particular social group. She argues that risk is intimately related to notions of politics, particularly in relation to accountability, responsibility and blame. She is also interested in how risk is a selective process: why some risks are ignored or downplayed while others are responded to with high anxiety, fear or anger.

Despite her emphasis on the importance of culture, Douglas demonstrates a 'weak' rather than a 'strong' constructionist (Chapter 2) approach to risk (a critical realist position). She argues that a range of risks or dangers exist in the real world, asserting that:

> [T]he reality of dangers is not at issue. The dangers are only too horribly real, in both cases, modern and pre-modern. This argument is not about the reality of dangers, but about how they are politicized. This point cannot be emphasized too much.
>
> (Douglas 1992: 29)

Certain dangers are selected from others for attention by a society and entitled 'risks' for certain reasons that make sense to a particular culture, based on its shared values and concerns. In other words, Douglas sees risk as a socially constructed interpretation and response to a 'real' danger that objectively exists, even if knowledge about it can only ever be mediated through sociocultural processes.

PURITY, DANGER AND THE BODY

Douglas' writings on risk build on ideas put forward in her earlier writings, particularly her influential work *Purity and Danger* (first published in 1966). In this book, an anthropological analysis of ideas and rituals concerning pollution and cleanliness in a range of societies is elaborated. Adopting a structuralist theoretical framework, Douglas set out to explain how taboos act in cultures to protect them from behaviours that threaten to destabilize them. As will be argued later in the chapter, Douglas' theorizing about purity, pollution and danger underpins her understanding of the cultural role and importance of risk in contemporary Western societies, particularly the use of risk as a concept for blaming and marginalizing an Other who is positioned as posing a threat (and thus a risk) to the integrity of self.

Central to Douglas' ideas about the symbolic nature of purity and pollution strategies is the insight that the human, fleshly body is a conceptual microcosm for the body politic (or the community of which it is a part). This is particularly the case in relation to how the flow of phenomena in and out of both bodies' openings is symbolically conceptualized and controlled and how boundaries between 'inside' and 'outside' are constructed and policed. Just as the human body is conceptualized as having certain boundaries between inside and outside, so too the notion of society sees it as having form, external boundaries, margins, internal structure:

> The body is a model which can stand for any bounded system. Its boundaries can represent any boundaries which are threatened or precarious. The body is a complex structure. The functions of its different parts and their relation afford a source of symbols for other complex structures.
>
> (Douglas 1966/1969: 115)

Notions of the body and its openings and boundaries address a major preoccupation of human societies: how to deal with the threats to order and stability posed by disorder, contamination and pollution.

For Douglas, bodily control is an expression of social control. If social controls over boundaries are relaxed, so too are controls over the openings of the individual's body. One of the central problematics of *Purity and Danger* was the identification of fixed systems by which notions of hygiene are understood and upon which they are acted. Thus, for example, ideas about what substances should be incorporated in the fleshly body – what is pure, and therefore safe, to ingest – mirror notions about the body politic and how the boundaries of a society are maintained, regulating the entry of certain types of people 'in' and keeping others 'outside' the body politic. Ideas about order and disorder fundamentally underlie beliefs about what is 'dirty' and what is 'clean'.

Classification systems in response to purity and contamination operate in all cultures. In some cultures, menstrual blood is considered especially defiling, while in others, death pollution is a constant preoccupation (Douglas 1966/1969: 121). In 'primitive' cultures, however, these classification systems have more force and totality, whereas in modern urbanized cultures, they are more fragmented and dispersed and thus hold less power (ibid.: 40). Pollution beliefs are therefore arbitrary, but within their own cultural context reflect deeper anxieties and fears.

Contemporary European notions of dirt and cleanliness, for example, are not so much the effect of concerns about micro-organisms than symbolic concerns, as

> [Dirt] is essentially disorder. There is no such thing as absolute dirt: it exists in the eye of the beholder. If we shun dirt, it is not because of craven fear, still less dread or holy terror. Nor do our ideas about disease account for the range of our behaviour in cleaning or avoiding dirt. Dirt offends against order. Eliminating it is not a negative movement, but a positive effort to organise the environment.
>
> (Douglas 1966/1969: 2)

Thus shoes are not dirty in themselves, but become dirty if placed on a dining table, because they are 'out of place'; food becomes dirt if bespattered on clothing or left on plates after eating is completed. Dirt is found to be offensive and disturbing because it threatens the 'proper' separateness of the individual from other things and people, it bespeaks intermingling, the breaking down of boundaries. It is particularly at the margins of the body/society that concerns and anxieties about purity and danger are directed. Because margins mark and straddle boundaries, they are liminal and therefore dangerous, requiring high levels of policing and control:

> All margins are dangerous. If they are pulled this way or that the shape of fundamental experience is altered. Any structure of ideas is vulnerable at its margins. We should expect the orifices of the body to symbolise its specially vulnerable points. Matter issuing from them is marginal stuff of the most obvious kind. Spittle, blood, milk, urine, faeces or tears by simply issuing forth have traversed the boundary of the body. So also have bodily parings, skin, nail, hair clippings and sweat. The mistake is to treat bodily margins in isolation from all other margins.
>
> (Douglas 1966/1969:121)

Rituals of purity and impurity serve to contain disorder, to support and bolster social ties, to 'create unity in experience' in particular cultural settings (Douglas 1966/1969: 2). Douglas gives the example of the Coorgs, a Hindu caste living in a mountainous region in India, who take great care in policing their body boundaries, treating the body 'as if it were a beleaguered town, every ingress and exit guarded for spies and traitors' (ibid.: 123). The Coorgs do not allow anything that issues from the body to re-enter it, for this is seen to be the most dangerous pollution. Their culture itself is isolated, having only occasional contact with the world around it. The Coorgs' obsession with policing the boundaries of their own bodies is mirrored in their anxiety about the contact that their community has with the outside, and the necessity of protecting the integrity, unity and survival of their minority group.

Ideas about pollution therefore operate at two levels of meaning. At the first level of meaning, which is largely instrumental, pollution ideas reinforce social pressures and rules, uphold moral values and support political power. Pollution ideas may be used as threats to maintain social order, to sanction the moral code; for example, linking disease to adultery or incest, a catastrophic weather event to political disloyalty (Douglas 1966/1969: 3). On a more symbolic level, pollution beliefs act as analogies for broader concerns about the social system, mirroring ideas about hierarchy or symmetry in social relations (ibid.: 5).

According to Douglas' schema, there are four kinds of social pollution within a social system or community. The first kind relates to a danger that threatens the external boundaries of the community, while the second comes from transgressing the internal boundaries of the community. The third kind of social pollution is engendered along the margins of boundaries, while the fourth is created by internal contradictions within the community 'when some of the basic postulates are denied by other basic postulates, so that at certain points the system seems to be at war with itself' (Douglas 1966/1969: 122). Pollution rules are often associated with moral codes. Indeed, pollution beliefs often serve to punish wrongdoing and thus support the moral system.

When moral principles lag, pollution beliefs can be used to bolster them by providing another rationale for disapproval. This may operate in four ways (ibid.: 133):

1. When a situation is morally ill-defined, a pollution belief can provide a rule for determining *post hoc* whether infraction has taken place, or not.

2. When moral principles come into conflict, a pollution rule can reduce confusion by giving a simple focus for concern.

3. When action that is held to be morally wrong does not provoke moral indignation, belief in the harmful consequences of a pollution can have the effect of aggravating the seriousness of the offence, and so of marshalling public opinion on the side of the right.

4. When moral indignation is not reinforced by practical sanctions, pollution beliefs can provide a deterrent to wrong-doers.

Douglas points out the special stigmatized and contaminating position of someone who is seen to transgress cultural boundaries: 'A polluting person is always in the wrong. He [*sic*] has developed some wrong condition or simply crossed some line which should not have been crossed and this displacement unleashes danger for someone' (1966/1969: 113). Polluting people, therefore, are seen as wicked, both because they have transgressed cultural norms or taboos and because they place others in danger by their actions.

All cultural classification systems have anomalies, things that do not fit, and ambiguities, things that may fit in more than one category. Anomalies and ambiguities are considered with anxiety, and are therefore treated as 'risky', or threatening. Douglas (1966/1969: 38) gives the example of treacle in Western societies. As a viscous substance, treacle breaches the border between the liquid and the solid. In its liminal status, its stickiness, the way in which it attacks the boundaries between Self and Other, treacle may be greeted with feelings of unease and repulsion. Slimy or oozing substances similarly evoke disgust.

All cultures have ways of dealing with these anomalies and ambiguities. One way to deal with ambiguity is to classify a phenomenon into one category only and maintain it within the category, thus reducing the potential for uncertainty. Another method of dealing with anomaly is to physically control it, removing it. A third way is to avoid anomalous things by strengthening and affirming the classification system that renders them anomalous. Alternatively, anomalous events or things may be labelled dangerous. Lastly, they may be dealt with by being used in ritual, as in poetry and mythology, 'to enrich meaning or call attention to other levels of existence' (Douglas 1966/1969: 40).

To summarize, the notion of 'dirt' and the related notions of 'contamination', 'pollution' and 'defilement' are inherently fraught with ideas about danger and risk. These notions spring from cultural concepts concerning boundaries, classifications and categories, the violation of which confounds cultural values and expectations. In this approach, 'risk' may be understood as the cultural response to transgression: the outcome of breaking a taboo, crossing a boundary, committing a sin. At the heart of these 'risks' are the emotional dimensions of transgression: anger, anxiety, frustration, hatred, rage, fear (see Chapter 7). As will be discussed in further detail in Chapter 8, transgression also evokes conflicting emotions and feelings, such as fascination, excitement and desire.

RISK AND BLAME

In her book *Risk Acceptability According to the Social Sciences* (1985), Douglas develops some of her insights from *Purity and Danger* in focusing directly on the sociocultural nature of risk. She therefore extends her earlier argument that 'humans pay attention to a particular pattern of disasters, treating them as omens or punishments' (ibid.: 2). In *Risk and Culture* (1982), written by Douglas with Aaron Wildavsky, the focus was primarily on Western societies' preoccupation with technological and environmental hazards.

Douglas (1985: 60) argues that in a situation where potential dangers dog one's every action and choice, the risks that receive most attention in a particular culture are those that are connected with legitimating moral principles. Like the distinctions drawn between dirty and pure objects or actions, danger is explained *qua* risk using cultural frames that are inevitably moral and political, and which rely on identifying responsibility for risk. In contemporary Western cultures, every death, every accident and every misfortune is 'chargeable to someone's account' – someone must be found to be blamed (Douglas 1992: 16):

> Whose fault? is the first question. Then, what action? Which means, what damages? what compensation? what restitution? and the preventive action is to improve the coding of risk in the domain which has turned out to be inadequately covered. Under the banner of risk reduction, a new blaming system has replaced the former combination of moralistic condemning the victim and opportunistic condemning the victim's incompetence.
>
> (ibid.)

The central tenet underlying cultural understandings of risk, therefore, is that 'in all places at all times the universe is moralized and politicized. Disasters that befoul the air and soil and poison the water are generally turned to political account: someone already unpopular is going to be blamed for it' (Douglas 1992: 5). This tenet underpins Douglas' discussions on the 'forensic theory of danger' (ibid.: 5–6), or how people, as members of certain social groups or communities, explain misfortune by looking back to what might have caused it. Here her earlier analyses of social pollution clearly influence her thinking. One type of explanation for misfortune, she argues, is moralistic and relates to a sin committed – someone died because they broke a taboo, and purification rituals are called for. Another explanation is that which attributes a misfortune to the work of individual adversaries. A third explanation blames the misfortune on an outside enemy, who must be punished.

In contemporary secularized societies, '[t]he concept of risk emerges as a key idea ... because of its uses as a forensic resource' (Douglas 1992: 24). Risk has largely replaced older ideas about the cause of misfortune. Concepts such as sin, which once were used to provide explanation for misfortune, are now discredited. In their place is the 'modern, sanitized discourse of risk' (ibid.: 26), which, despite its apparent scientific neutrality, reinterprets 'sins' as 'risks' and functions in the same way as a moral discourse. The difference between danger in the context of taboo as it is used in pre-modern societies and risk as a central concept of danger in modern societies is that taboo is tied into rhetorics of retribution and accusation against a specific individual. As such, it is a means of binding a community together by ensuring that norms and boundaries are maintained. In contrast, the concept of risk, as part of a more individualistic community, is invoked to protect individuals against others: 'The dialogue about risk plays the role equivalent to taboo or sin, but the slope is tilted in the reverse direction, away from protecting the community and in favour of protecting the individual' (ibid.: 28). Being nominated as 'at risk', Douglas argues,

> is not the equivalent but the reciprocal of being 'in sin' or 'under taboo'. To be 'at risk' is equivalent to being sinned against, being vulnerable to the events caused by others, whereas being 'in sin' means being the cause of harm.
>
> (1992: 28)

Being 'at risk', in other words, entails being placed in the role of victim, threatened by risks imposed upon oneself by other agents, rather than being seen as bringing risk upon oneself through one's own actions.

Douglas (1992) asks why it is that the word 'risk' has come to prominence at this point of Western history, replacing concepts such as danger. Her answer is that it is not simply a matter of risk having claims to be 'scientific', although this is an important aspect of the process. Rather, risk concerns have emerged as part of a complex of new ideas, incorporating a heightened sensitivity to issues of danger. Douglas sees the current concern with risk as a product of globalization, which has resulted in a new level of inter-community discourse and a sense of vulnerability in being part of a world system. As a consequence of globalization, the nation has to provide new kinds of protection. In this context:

> The idea of risk could have been custom-made. Its universalizing terminology, its abstractness, its power of condensation, its scientificity, its connection with objective analysis, make it perfect. Above all, its forensic uses fit the tool to the task of building a culture that supports a modern industrial society.
>
> (Douglas 1992: 15)

According to Douglas, this 'new concern with risk' is part of 'a public backlash against the great corporations' (ibid.: 15). The political pressure that is brought to bear in relation to risk disputes is largely against exposing others to risk. This pressure is therefore centred less on individuals as being to blame and more on large organizations. In remarking on the ways in which social organizations such as the green movement respond to risk, Douglas points to the political and moralistic nature of risk discourses:

> Though the public seems to be thinking politically in terms of comparative risks, the number-crunching does not matter; the idea of risk is transcribed simply as unacceptable danger. So 'risk' does not signify an all-round assessment of probable outcomes but becomes a stick for beating authority, often a slogan for mustering xenophobia.
>
> (1992: 39)

Douglas and Wildavsky (1982) explain the influence of environmental activists in debates over the risks associated with ecological degradation and pollution in terms of the environmental movement having a secular sect-like nature. To achieve internal cohesiveness, they claim, the environmental movement positions an Other – in this case, particular industries and government departments – as the enemy that is demonized and blamed for risk.

Imputations of risk, therefore, like those of impurity, may be used as a means of social coercion and maintaining the moral and social order, a way of dealing with 'polluting people' who are culturally positioned as on the margins of society. This positioning occurs not just with organizations but also with social groups and individuals. Certain classes of people are singled out as likely victims of hazards, as being 'at risk' and therefore requiring control to bring them back to conforming to moral values. If the blame is removed from the victims and placed on the shoulders of their close kin, the tendency towards moral conformity is even more effective, as when parents are blamed for a child's disability (Douglas 1985: 57).

Here, despite Douglas' insistence, discussed above, that being 'at risk' is different from being 'in sin', it can be seen that people may sometimes be blamed for being 'at risk' just as they were once blamed for being 'in sin'. Blame may also be located externally, upon enemies, as a means of diverting attention away from oneself. Each type of strategy tends to be used in different contexts, albeit for the same purpose: to maintain social cohesion:

> Clearly, blaming the victim is a strategy that works in one kind of context, and blaming the outside enemy, a strategy that works in another. Victim blaming facilitates social control; outsider blaming enhances loyalty. Both ploys would serve as an intention to prevent the community from being riven by dissension.
>
> (Douglas 1985: 59)

THE GRID-GROUP MODEL

Another important feature of Douglas' structuralist cultural theory is her attempt to distinguish between certain defined modes of organization and their related responses to risk. Douglas (1985: 61–3) defines two different ideal-types of social organization in terms of their dominant approach to risk. The first is that in which the members have a strong commitment to strengthening and maintaining internal bonds. To this end, they institute sharply defined separations within a hierarchy and close the community against the outside. This type of community prefers to allocate responsibility for disaster to victims and their kin, along with strategies for them to repent and expiate their sins. It is therefore both morally punitive and conciliatory. The second type of social organization has a strong commitment to individual enterprise and fair competition, and thus is founded on internal conflict rather than solidarity. This heroic, adversarial community has a more neutral approach to disasters, based on notions of chance and fate rather than culpability and punishment.

In other writings, this dichotomy is expanded to present a four-cell model of risk rationalities or worldviews. With Wildavsky, Douglas developed the 'grid-group' model of behaviour in understanding different logics of risk as they are expressed in social groups or organizations (Douglas and Wildavsky 1982; Douglas 1992). The group index contrasts two ideal-types of groups: those who have a high group ethos and those with a low group ethos. This index refers to 'the outside boundary that people have erected between themselves and the outside world' (Douglas and Wildavsky

1982: 138). The high group ethos emphasizes cohesion among group members and makes strong distinctions between 'us' (members of the group) and 'them' (the world outside the group), while the low group ethos emphasizes individuality and weaker ties with others. The grid index relates to 'all the other social distinctions and delegations of authority that [people] use to limit how people behave to one another' (ibid.: 138). These include the extent of social constraints on individual behaviour, imposed either by group membership or by other structural factors such as gender, ethnicity/race and social class. Individuals in groups classified as ideal type 'high grid' are subject to a large number of cultural constraints, while those who are 'low grid' have few constraints shaping their actions.

Putting these two indices together, four ideal-types and consonant four approaches to risk can be identified. They include: *hierarchists* (high group and high grid) who respect authority, conform closely to group norms and expectations relating to risk and trust established organizations; *egalitarians* (high group and low grid) who strongly identify with their group and blame outsiders for risk, tending to be distrustful of externally imposed norms and supportive of social equality issues and a participatory approach to risk; *individualists* (low group and low grid), who are individualistic and entrepreneurial, support self-regulation of risk, trust individuals rather than organizations, believe in market forces, see risk-taking as bringing benefits as well as dangers with it and resent external constraints; and *fatalists* (low group and high grid) who lack strong cohesion to a group but are otherwise highly constrained in their behaviours, and tend to trust to luck and fate in relation to risk, seeing themselves as having little personal control over it (Douglas and Wildavsky 1982).

This model may be subject to criticism for its apparent rigidness, static nature and inability to account for the ways in which most individuals constantly move between the four worldviews rather than belonging to one or the other. It tends to treat the concept of 'risk' as a given in suggesting that it is the worldview rather than the nature of the risk itself that is the source of differential responses to risk. Yet it may be argued that worldviews themselves shape which phenomena are singled out as 'risks' and how serious they are perceived as being. They are therefore complicit in the production of risks and not simply responses to given risks. Nonetheless, if it is accepted that the model presents ideal-types rather than assuming that people can be accurately identified as belonging and adhering to only one of the four worldviews, it provides a basis for examining the cultural locations within which risk is conceptualized and dealt with in a particular sociocultural setting.

The grid-group approach has been used across a diverse range of research: for example, to review the literature on the causes of the banking crisis and associated global economic recession of 2008–2010 (Hindmoor 2010), to categorize perspectives on punishment in the criminal justice system (Vaughan 2002) and analyse lay views on pandemic influenza resource allocation (Docter *et al.* 2011). It has been frequently used in social psychology as a basis for exploring cultural differences (often termed 'cultural biases') in worldviews and how these structure risk perceptions (Olofsson and Rashid 2011).

Douglas (1992) has used the grid-group to explore the ways in which a particular city or town may include four types of groups, all of which have different responses to a threat such as HIV/AIDS. Building on her previous assertions about the relationship between notions of the human body and those of the body politic, she relates the group response to HIV/AIDS risk to specific conceptualizations of the individual body. She describes four abstract conceptualizations of the body in relation to the threat of illness and disease found among residents in Brittany, a region of France. The first conceptualizes the body as porous, completely open to the invasion of infection and therefore not able to protect itself against illness. The second is a vision of the body as very strong, with an immune system that is resistant to infection and thus requiring little in the way of protection apart from engagement in hygienic routines that allow it to function well. The third is a conceptualization of the body as having two protective layers, its own physical skin and the community, each of which acts to police entries and exits and thus the risk of contamination to the individual body. The fourth is a concept of the body as a machine that has its own protective envelope, which if pierced through an act of carelessness (for example, allowing penetration by an infected person's bodily fluids) renders the body susceptible to infection.

In each conceptualization of the body, HIV/AIDS risk is viewed differently. For the first conceptualization, risk is ever-present and difficult to guard against, but for this reason, those who become infected are not seen as being to blame. For the second, risk is a minor problem, because the body is regarded as inherently so resistant to infection. The third conceptualization sees risk prevention as directed at guarding the boundaries of the two protective layers, particularly monitoring the boundaries of the community.

For the fourth, risk is engendered by lack of proper care of the body and therefore those who succumb to infection are viewed as lacking appropriate self-regulation. Education about the transmission routes of HIV infection often founders in the face of these cultural models of the body.

Douglas (1992) then explores four typologies of city groups that reflect the conceptualizations of the body described above. The first is the city core or the central community, a hierarchical structure which dominates the city and defends its centrality against outsiders. In the face of an epidemic such as HIV/AIDS, the city core tightens its defences, adopting hygienic measures proposed by experts. It adopts the model of the community as having two skins, a double protective envelope of bodily defence and community defence against invasion. The core group therefore ranges all its forces against the external threat, which is seen to emerge from among those who deviate from the moral order, such as gay men, prostitutes, injecting drug users. The second group is that of the dissenting minorities, who are not organized hierarchically but through solidarity in their protest against the dominant city core group, whom they position as oppressive of their agency. This group rejects the expert knowledge of the core group, often engaging in self-help or alternative strategies. In the case of HIV/AIDS, such groups may include gay community groups and AIDS activist groups. They also adopt the model of the community as having a double protective envelope, seeing the body as needing to protect itself from infection and the community as having to guard itself from outsiders who may contaminate it. This minority community, however, unlike the core community, is inherently defined as unhealthy and diseased, for it is characterized by having many members who are ill with HIV/AIDS (hence their marginalization from the core). Members of the dissenting enclave may therefore sometimes have a fatalistic approach to HIV risk.

The third group is individualist, comprising of individuals adopting the culture of entrepreneurialism who operate as autonomous units and resist being defined as part of a community. Those in this group want to be left free to pursue their own interests. They tend to be idiosyncratic in their response to risk advice. They see themselves as being in control of the routes of infection to the extent that they want to be, and often scorn the importance of engaging in precautionary strategies such as safer sex activities. The fourth group is the isolate or fatalist group, a residual category expelled to the margins by the centre community. They rather unwillingly find themselves restricted by the structures imposed by others. They tend not to respond as active agents to HIV/AIDS risk, but instead accept whatever fate might bring them. Unfortunately Douglas (1992) is not explicit about which of the models of the body these latter two groups might favour in terms of HIV/AIDS risk, but it is clearly not that of the double envelope of protection, as these groups would not think in terms of community membership. Rather, risk-taking would be conceptualized at the level of one's own deportment of the body and interaction with others' bodies. It seems likely that these groups may adopt any of the other three models of the body described by Douglas, as each of these models is individualistic, relying on individuals to take their own actions to protect themselves from risk.

This analysis has something to offer, particularly in bringing together models of the human body in relation to HIV/AIDS with those of the body politic. The way in which dominant social groups have reacted against those they have positioned as 'deviant' and 'risky' by attempting to marginalize and exclude them, drawing up a *cordon sanitaire* of hygienic strategies to demarcate boundaries, is a clear trend in the history of the HIV/AIDS epidemic (and many other infectious diseases) in most societies (see Chapter 7 for further elaboration on strategies that define Self against Other in response to risk.) Again, however, this model may be criticized for being rather too static and general in its categorizations, not acknowledging the heterogeneity of social groups. Gay men, for example, even those who are members of AIDS activist groups, do not all necessarily reject the expert advice issuing forth from the core community and turn towards self-help remedies. Indeed, many activist groups have called for more rather than less advice and therapeutic treatment from mainstream medicine.

CONCLUDING COMMENTS

Mary Douglas' theoretical approach to risk has been influential because she has provided a trenchant and persuasive critique of the naïve realist approaches that have dominated the fields of risk analysis and risk perception. Her 'cultural/symbolic' approach emphasizes that risk judgements are political, moral and aesthetic, constructed through cultural frameworks of understanding and implicated with notions of the body and the importance of establishing and maintaining conceptual boundaries. This provides a perspective on risk that sets up an important counterpoint to the individualist focus that predominates in the naïve realist technico-scientific approaches. For those interested in questions of risk that go beyond the individualistic to a fundamentally shared, cultural and symbolic approach to risk, Douglas' writings provide a firm basis. Her approach does tend to be somewhat static, however, as is typical of functional structuralist analyses of sociocultural phenomena. There is little explanation provided for how things might change in Douglas' accounts of risk, purity and danger.

There is also somewhat of a problem in the way that Douglas' theorizing on risk has been used by others. As pointed out in Chapter 1, a number of researchers from such fields as psychology have begun to incorporate some of Douglas' insights into their models of risk perception, often referring to her work as the 'cultural theory' approach to risk. In this literature, however, Douglas' writings are frequently interpreted as implying that lay perceptions of risk involve inaccuracies and errors of judgement because of the 'contaminating' influence of cultural and social processes. In an article on people's perceptions of the risk of crime, for example, Kemshall uses Douglas and other cultural theorists to support her claim that

> Risk perception can be prone to bias and error leading to exaggeration and overestimation of risks. Risk perception is a subjective process, with what we identify and respond to as a risk often a matter of value judgement rather than fact.
>
> (1997: 247–8)

In such writings, as in much of the other technico-scientific literature on risk assessment and risk perception, the risk judgement of 'experts' continue to be privileged as 'objective' and 'factual' over those of lay people, against which perceptions are compared and found wanting.

Other commentators who take a *laissez-faire* political approach have used Douglas' work to claim that the state should not attempt to impose its views on risk on the public in risk reduction efforts, given the 'subjective' nature of risk assessment, the uncertainty of knowledge about risk and the political dimensions of risk debates (see, for example, Adams 1995). Douglas' own position on risk sometimes seems to support a politically conservative approach, particularly in her writings on the environmentalist movement. Douglas and her collaborator Wildavsky have been criticized for siding with business and industry inappropriately by positioning them as the victims of the environmental movement. One reviewer of *Risk and Culture,* for example, has seen their ideas as seeming 'to proceed more from an animus against environmentalism and middle-class "liberalism" than from Douglas's work on pollution' (Kaprow 1985: 345). In Douglas and Wildavsky's work, environmentalists tend to be portrayed as behaving politically and ideologically, in constructing certain beliefs about industrial pollution and risk. In contrast, the risk positions of industry and big business tend to be represented as politically neutral. In this respect, therefore, and in representing industry and big business as singled out as scapegoats and inappropriately blamed for risk, Douglas may herself be criticized for failing to recognize the cultural underpinnings of these institutions' risk positions. This seems to clash with her overall position on risk, which while taking a 'weak' rather than 'strong' social constructionist approach, is adamant about the inherently cultural nature of any group or community's perceptions and judgements about risk.

4

RISK AND REFLEXIVE MODERNIZATION

As I observed in Chapter 2, the exponents of the 'risk society' perspective are primarily interested in the ways in which the concept of risk is related to the conditions of late modernity. This perspective offers an approach that considers the politics and macro-level of the current meanings and strategies of risk. 'Risk society' exponents focus on such processes as individualization, reflexivity and globalization as converging in the 'risk society' of Western nations. This chapter examines the insights offered by the two major exponents of the 'risk society' thesis: Ulrich Beck and Anthony Giddens. Although they initially developed their diagnoses of risk and late modernity largely separately of each other, the writings of Beck and Giddens have much in common: hence the decision to consider them together in this chapter. However, as I note at the end of the chapter, there are also some major differences in their writings which require acknowledgment.

BECK AND THE 'RISK SOCIETY'

The German sociologist Ulrich Beck has become a prominent figure in the sociological literature on risk. His book *Risk Society: Towards a New Modernity* was first published in English translation in 1992 (the original German version appeared six years previously) and sparked much debate about the nature of risk in contemporary Western societies. Since then, Beck followed up this book with others on aspects on risk, many of which are available in English. These works include *Reflexive Modernization* (1994, written with Anthony Giddens and Scott Lash), *The Normal Chaos of Love* (1995, written with Elisabeth Beck-Gernsheim), *Ecological Politics in the Age of Risk* (1995), *World Risk Society* (1999), *The Cosmopolitan Vision* (2006) and *World at Risk* (2009a), as well as many journal articles and book chapters on the subject. As the titles of these books suggest, Beck has increasingly focused on the concepts of 'world risk society' and 'cosmopolitanism', both of which involve the consequences of globalization on risk and relations between nation-states.

In his earlier publications, Beck set out his argument that individuals in contemporary Western societies were living in a transitional period, in which industrial society was becoming a 'risk society'. In this transitional period, the production of wealth was accompanied by that of risks, which have proliferated as an outcome of modernization. The central problem of Western societies, therefore, was not the production and distribution of 'goods' such as wealth and employment in conditions of scarcity (as it was in early modernity and remains the case in developing countries) but the prevention or minimization of 'bads', that is, risks. Debates and conflicts over risks had begun to dominate public, political and private arenas. Individuals living in these societies had therefore moved towards a greater awareness of risk and were forced to deal with risks on an everyday basis.

For Beck, 'risk', is another word for a hazard or danger, and he claims that the 'risks of modernization' are 'irreversible threats to the life of plants, animals, and human beings' (Beck 1992b: 13). At many points he demonstrates anger at the ever-hazardous nature of life in late modernity, presenting an apocalyptic vision of how hazards and dangers may destroy humankind and other living creatures. In some parts of Beck's work, the social and cultural processes by which understandings and perceptions of risk are mediated are highlighted, and he thus demonstrates a 'weak' version of social constructionism or a critical realist approach. In *Ecological Politics in the Age of Risk* (1995), Beck contrasts what he sees as the two major approaches to interpreting risk: 'natural-scientific objectivism about hazards' (Beck's term for the naïve realist approach) and 'cultural relativism about hazards' (his term for the 'strong' social constructionist approach). He sees both approaches as having their strengths and weaknesses. 'Natural-scientific objectivism' is useful, he argues, because it identifies risks using technical powers of observation, measurement and calculation. The weakness of objectivism, however, is that in its quest for neutral objectivity, it fails to recognize the ways in which 'scientific facts', like other views on risk, are situated and interpreted in cultural and political contexts.

The 'cultural relativism' approach, in Beck's view, appropriately emphasizes the contextual aspect of risk responses.

Risk calculations, from this perspective, 'are now no longer thought of as arbitrators but as protagonists in the confrontation, which is enacted in terms of percentages, experimental results, projections, etc.' (Beck 1995: 92). Yet he sees this approach as often becoming too relativist, regarding anything as potentially classifiable as dangerous, according to the viewpoint that is taken, and failing to recognize the special nature of 'real' contemporary hazards. Beck seeks to integrate both approaches into what he calls 'a sociological perspective' (ibid.: 76). He maintains a 'natural-scientific objectivist' approach by subscribing to the idea that 'real' risks exist, but brings in 'cultural relativism' (in other words, a 'weak' social constructionist or critical realist position) by arguing that the nature and causes of risks are conceptualized and dealt with differently in contemporary Western societies compared with previous eras. Beck (1999) argues that one should not have to choose between one or the other but rather should use each when it is appropriate to understand the complex and ambivalent nature of risk.

Beck is interested in the 'cultural disposition' demonstrated by individuals and social groups to single out certain risks as important while others are ignored. He asks, for example, why it is that the problem of the 'dying forests' is given such attention (particularly in his country, Germany) when other hazards, such as mass death on the roads, are largely ignored? The reason is that such events 'touch a culture nerve' for some reason, while others do not and thus do not attract alarm (Beck 1995: 47). Thus, images of dying seals or forests come to stand for the vastness of the risks that surround us, rendering comprehensible the incomprehensible and giving us a target on which to fix an illusory sense of control. The usual response to grave dangers is to deny their existence as a kind of psychological self-protective mechanism, an attempt to maintain a sense of normality. Symbolic targets of contamination help us do this by focusing our attentions toward them and ignoring other risks (ibid.: 48–9).

Beck acknowledges that all societies in all epochs in human history have been subject to threats to health and life, and therefore could be described as 'risk societies'. However, he reserves the term 'risk society' to describe exclusively the trends of the contemporary era. Beck singles out for examination the risks in three eras: (1) pre-modern societies; (2) early modern; and (3) contemporary, or late modern societies (also referred to in his work as pre-industrialism, early industrialism and late industrialism). He identifies several distinct features of risk in late compared with early modernity. A major difference is that dangers and hazards in contemporary societies – principally environmental problems such as air and water pollution, ionizing radiation and toxic chemicals in foodstuffs – differ significantly from previous eras. Since the middle of the twentieth century, Beck claims, industrial society has been confronted with threats to human life which are on an unprecedented scale. Such threats cannot be delimited spatially, temporally or socially, unlike the 'personal' risks produced by early industrialization. The magnitude and global nature of risks are such that risks are becoming more and more difficult to quantify, prevent and avoid. Contemporary hazards now are often open-ended events, rather than events that have a foreseeable end. Beck talks about 'higher and higher levels of hazard' becoming 'the norm' (Beck 1995: 13). In the contemporary era, he argues, hazards are far more apocalyptic than in previous eras, threatening the destruction of all life on Earth.

Beck also contrasts the calculability of contemporary hazards with those of previous eras. He compares ways of thinking about and dealing with threats and hazards in pre-modern societies with those of early modernity. In pre-modern society, common threats (plague, famine, natural catastrophes, wars, but also magic, gods, demons) were deemed incalculable because they were attributed to external, supernatural causes. Via the processes of modernity taking place in early industrialism, however, these threats were transformed into calculable risks in the course of the development of instrumental rational control (Beck 1995: 30). 'Risks' as they were understood in early modernity, were 'determinable, calculable uncertainties', seen as 'products of social choice, which must be weighed against opportunities and acknowledged, dealt with, or simply foisted on individuals' (ibid.: 77).

According to Beck, in the late modern era the foundations of risk logic as it was developed in early modernity are being subverted or suspended. The processes of modernist risk calculation fail in the 'risk society'. The risks of late modern society are not easily calculable because of their non-localized nature and potential long-term effects: 'to express it by reference to a single example: the injured of Chernobyl are today, years after the catastrophe, not even born yet' (Beck 1996a: 31). In the event of the worst possible disaster or accident (such as from nuclear, biological or chemical weapons of mass destruction), the effects of which are long-lasting, irreparable and incalculable, there is no institution which could prevent it or compensate for its effects.

In such a scenario, it is difficult to identify a single cause upon which blame can be cast or to award financial compensation for the damage done, given the magnitude of the threat (ibid.: 15). The established early modernist rules of attribution and causality, therefore, break down in the face of the globalization of risk, as do the safety systems that once dealt with risk, such as insurance and compensation arrangements. Contemporary hazards can only be minimized by technological means – they can never be removed entirely (Beck 1995: 76–7).

In 'risk society' the assessment of risk is subject to a high degree of ambivalence, due to the complexity of society and technical knowledge. In the early days of industrialization, risks and hazards were evident to the senses – they could be smelt, touched, tasted or observed with the naked eye. In contrast, many of the major risks today largely escape perception, for they are 'localized in the sphere of physical and chemical formulas (e.g. toxins in foodstuffs or the nuclear threat)' (Beck 1992b: 21). These risks exist in scientific knowledge rather than in everyday experience. Expert knowledges tend to contradict each other, resulting in debates over standpoints, calculation procedures and results. This also tends to paralyze action. Science itself fails in response to the large-scale, indeterminate nature of contemporary hazards. Hypotheses about their safety cannot be tested empirically and science has little power to intervene in a context in which the world has become a laboratory for testing how hazards affect populations. Scientists have therefore lost their authority in relation to risk assessments: scientific calculations are challenged more and more by political groups and activists (Beck 1995: 125–6).

The nature of such hazards therefore returns the concept of risk to the pre-modern notion of 'incalculable insecurities'. In common with such hazards, they 'undercut the social logic of risk calculation and provision' (Beck 1995: 77). Ways of viewing and dealing with contemporary hazards are not the same as pre-modern viewpoints, however. The notion of 'nature', the demons or acts of God that frightened individuals in pre-modern societies, is a supernatural concept. 'Nature', and its dangers, were then seen as imposed by external forces and thus beyond the control of humans. By contrast, dangers and hazards in early and late modern societies are seen as humanly generated rather than supernatural. They are thus considered the responsibility of humans to control and in principle can be avoided or altered.

This raises another important distinction between 'older dangers' and contemporary hazards – the linking of human responsibility with the latter. Because contemporary hazards are seen to be the outcome of human action – principally the related events of modernization, industrialization, urbanization and globalization – the drawbacks of such events are continually confronted and challenged. While uncertainties may always have been part of life, the difference in late modernity is that many of them arise from (rather than being assuaged by) the very growth in human knowledge. Indeed, even older risks such as plagues, floods and famines, are now rarely viewed as acts of gods or demons or the result of 'nature gone wrong'. Instead, human intervention is seen to have played a major role, resulting in nature 'striking back' for having been so cruelly treated or inappropriately managed.

Thus, for example, epidemics of bacterial infections are blamed on medicines resulting in antibiotic-resistant bacteria, the cause of floods, landslides and famines are traced back to the over-clearing of land and weather changes due to global warming, which in turn is seen to be the side-effect of industrialization. Risks, in their contemporary meaning, are fundamentally based on decisions, principally made by organizations and political groups, which consider techno-economic advantages and considerations of utility. As a result, 'it is not the number of dead and wounded, but rather a social feature, their industrial self-generation, which makes the hazards of mega-technology a political issue' (Beck 1992a: 98).

REFLEXIVE MODERNIZATION

The political aspects of risk and the self-critique that is inspired by risk are pivotal to Beck's concept of risk society. He defines risk as

a systematic way of dealing with hazards and insecurities induced and introduced by modernization itself. Risks, as opposed to older dangers, are consequences which relate to the threatening force of modernization and to its globalization of doubt. They are politically reflexive.

(Beck 1992b: 21)

The concept of risk is linked to reflexivity because anxieties about risks serve to pose questions about current practices. In risk society, society becomes reflexive in three ways, stemming from the newly global nature of risk. First, society becomes an issue and a problem for itself at the global level. Second, the awareness of the global nature of risk triggers new impulses towards the development of cooperative international institutions. Third, the boundaries of the political come to be removed, leading to worldwide alliances (Beck 1996a).

Beck (1994, 1996b) contends that the use of the term 'reflexive' in his concept of reflexive modernization does not denote mere 'reflection' but rather 'self-confrontation'. The move towards reflexivity is an unintended side-effect of modernity, or rather the hazards produced by modernity as part of its project (1996b: 28). It is the process of modernity coming to examine and critique itself. It is thus not a repudiation of modernity *per se* but rather an application of the principles of modernity to itself. Reflexive modernization contains two phases. The first (the reflex stage) is part of the automatic transition from industrial to risk society, where risks are produced as part of the processes of modernization but are not yet the subject of sustained public or personal debate or political conflict. The second (the reflection stage) involves industrial society coming to see itself as a risk society, with the growing realization of the dangers involved in modernity which then calls into question the structures of society. Reflexive modernization, therefore, is:

> the combination of reflex and reflections which, as long as the catastrophe itself fails to materialise, can set industrial modernity on the path to self-criticism and self-transformation. Reflexive modernisation contains both elements: the reflex-like threat to industrial society's own foundations through a successful further modernisation which is blind to dangers, *and* the growth of awareness, the reflection on this situation.
>
> (Beck 1996b: 34, original emphasis)

This critical reflection upon the dangers of modernity is the difference between industrial society and risk society.

For Beck, reflexive modernization leads to the 'possibility of a creative (self)-destruction for an entire epoch: that of industrial society' (1994: 2). Progress has turned into self-destruction, but not through class struggle or revolution, as Marx predicted, but as an unintended consequence, through the inexorable and incremental processes of modernization itself. Judgements on risk represent implicit moral judgements (albeit masked in the discourse of objective, quantitative 'facts'), on the ways in which human societies have developed (Beck 1992b: 176). The naïve certainties of the Enlightenment – the optimism in human progress wrought through science and rationalized action – have disintegrated, resulting in individuals' need to seek and invent new certainties for themselves (Beck 1994: 14). Lay people have become sceptical about science, because they are aware that science has produced many of the risks about which they are concerned and that scientific knowledge about risk is incomplete and often contradictory, failing to solve the problems it has created. People must deal, therefore, with constant insecurity and uncertainty: conventional social order seems to be breaking down in the face of the undermining of old certainties. There is a continual definitional struggle over risk, particularly between those who produce risk definitions (principally experts) and those who consume them (the lay public). In risk society, as a result, risk has become a highly political concept.

Beck (1992b: 59) is critical of experts' positioning of lay people as ignorant, merely requiring more information about risk to respond appropriately. He argues that lay people's apparent 'irrationality' in relation to risk is a highly rational response to the failure of technico-scientific rationality in the face of the growing risks of late modernity. The understandable response of individuals is to become critical of these dangers generated by early modernity and its drive towards industrial production. Beck claims that this is already happening in diverse forms in organizations such as the green movement but also among members of the general public.

Beck somewhat confusingly sees risk as simultaneously reinforcing positions of inequity and as democratizing, creating a global citizenship. He acknowledges that some social groups are more affected than others by the distribution and growth of risks, and these differences may be structured through inequalities of class and social position. The disadvantaged have fewer opportunities to avoid risks because of their lack of resources compared with the advantaged: 'Poverty attracts an unfortunate abundance of risks. By contrast, the wealthy (in income, power or education), can purchase safety and freedom from risk' (Beck 1992b: 35). Beck also points to growing inequalities in risk distribution, where class positions and risk positions overlap. He acknowledges that what he calls 'the former colonies' of the Western world are on their way to becoming the waste-dumps of the world for toxic and nuclear wastes produced by more privileged countries (ibid.).

However, Beck also argues that many of the risks of risk society affect the wealthy and the poor in similar ways: 'poverty is hierarchic, smog is democratic' (Beck 1992b: 36). Such risks as radiation, nuclear warfare, toxic chemicals in food and air and water pollution, because they are so widespread and 'invisible' in their manifestations or effects, or both, cannot be avoided even by those who are socio-economically advantaged. The risks of modernization also affect those who have produced or profited from them, breaking down boundaries between classes and countries. One feature of risk society is that those individuals who are most concerned and aware about risks are from the highly educated, well-off classes, because they make great efforts to inform themselves about risks. Despite their best attempts, however, these people's knowledge about the extent of risk is incomplete, for they do not have access to scientific knowledge (that owned by 'external knowledge producers', ibid.: 53). Risk society is thus characterized by the contradiction that the privileged have greater access to knowledge, but not enough, so that they become anxious without being able to reconcile or act upon their anxiety.

INDIVIDUALIZATION

The concept of individualization is also central to Beck's view of risk society and reflexive modernization. Individualization refers not to alienation or loneliness. Instead it means the requirement in late modernity that individuals must produce their own biographies themselves, in the absence of fixed, obligatory and traditional norms and certainties and the emergence of new ways of life that are continually subject to change (Beck 1994: 13). Individualization is the other, private side of globalization in reflexive modernization. The core of reflexive modernity is a transformation in and freeing of accepted social roles such as gender and social class (Beck 1992b: 87ff.). Beck sees individualization as the outcome of modernization processes involving a reduction in the influence of the traditional structuring institutions of society in the formation of personal identity. Such factors as mass education, improvements in living standards, the second-wave feminist movement and changes in the labour market have contributed to the trend towards individualization.

Individualization means 'the disintegration of the certainties of industrial society as well as the compulsion to find and invent new certainties for oneself and others without them' (Beck 1994: 14). It is dependent on decision-making as it assumes agency, the ability to shape one's destiny through self-determination and identification. There has been 'a social surge of individualisation' (Beck 1992b: 87) in which people have become compelled to make themselves the centre of the conduct of life, taking on multiple and mutable subjectivities. Individualization is a social transformation that is complex and ambiguous: 'Seen from one angle it means freedom to choose, and from another pressure to conform to internalized demands, on the one hand being responsible for yourself and on the other being dependent on conditions which completely elude your grasp' (Beck and Beck-Gernsheim 1995: 7). While, as a long-term outcome of social processes, individualization does not affect all social groups similarly, it has had an increasing effect on the conduct of everyday life for large numbers of people.

Where once, in pre-modern society, it was expected that one's destiny was pre-structured through the chance of one's station in life at birth, the life course is now conceptualized as far more flexible and open, albeit through individual's endeavours rather than the vagaries of fortune. Beck (1992b: 135) refers to this as 'reflexive biography', or biography that is self-produced rather than socially produced. Traditional forms of coping with anxiety and insecurity – families, marriage and male–female roles – are failing, and individuals must turn to themselves, creating new demands for social institutions such as education, counselling, therapy and politics (ibid.: 153).

Individualization, therefore, involves a proliferation of new demands upon people at the same time as choices have become more and more complex and difficult, particularly in relation to such matters as sexual identity, work and family relationships. Such planning requires a high and continuing exertion of reflexivity upon the nature and future of one's life course. In such arenas as education and work, for example, people are expected to make their destinies, to compete with others for credentials and employment and make their individualized careers, no longer relying on traditional expectations or social structures. Stable employment can no longer be taken as a given, and it is considered up to people to make their own opportunities. Workers must deal with a pluralized, decentralized labour market which makes demands of them to be flexible and entrepreneurial, or else suffer the consequences of under-employment or unemployment.

In the arena of personal relationships, individualization results in greater conflict between individuals in intimate partnerships, as each attempts to pursue her or his right for autonomy and self-improvement as well as maintain a relationship. Gender roles no longer rigidly structure the life course. As a result, there are greater possibilities for choice in the conduct of relationships, but this has required intense and continual negotiation and decision-making for couples. People must juggle their need for autonomy and self-expression with their need for dependence and emotional stability in relationships. Contradictions have opened up between the demands of the family and those of the workplace, which assumes an autonomous individual who is unburdened with family responsibilities. In this context, new personal risks have been generated, particularly for women, involving insecurities around employment and economic issues as well as around the stability of relationships in marriage (Beck and Beck-Gernsheim 1995).

Individualization is therefore fraught with risk, according to Beck. With the breakdown of many of the traditional certainties structured through age, gender and social class, a plurality of new risks are generated, including unemployment or under-employment, marital instability and family breakdown, accompanied by high levels of anxiety and insecurity. Life becomes less certain even while it is placed more under one's control. This move towards individualization does not mean that social inequalities or structuring of opportunities through such attributes as class, gender or ethnicity have disappeared. Rather, in the face of individualization, the influence of these structures has become less obvious and acknowledged as affecting life chances. Inequalities have become primarily viewed as individualized, perceived as 'psychological dispositions: as personal inadequacies, guilt feelings, anxieties, conflicts, and neuroses' (Beck 1992b: 100). To choose the wrong kind of university degree, occupation or marriage partner, to face unemployment or marital breakdown, tends to be considered the result of an individual's faulty planning or decision-making rather than the outcome of broader social processes.

WORLD RISK SOCIETY AND COSMOPOLITANISM

In his earlier writings on risk society, Beck noted that via the processes of risk modernization, risk society has become 'world risk society', in which the public sphere of political debate and action is globalized. World risk society has produced a different kind of citizenship, 'global citizenship', in which the traditional means of defining identity, based on local contexts, are exchanged for a focus on the worldwide perspective. This perspective has resulted in the generation of new alliances, of *ad hoc* activist groups, a new and different form of politics beyond traditional hierarchies (Beck 1996a: 2).

Since the turn of this century, Beck has begun focusing more attention on describing the nature of world risk society, and has introduced the concept of the 'cosmopolitan turn'. While his original writings on risk society tended to focus particularly on environmental risks but also to a lesser extent those associated with employment and unemployment and with the family, in his more recent work Beck (2009a, 2009b, 2011) singles out three axis of conflict in contemporary world risk society: (1) environmental risk conflicts (particularly climate change); (2) global financial risks; and (3) terrorism risks; the latter two of which are relatively new.

Beck's (2002, 2006, 2009b, 2011, 2012; Beck and Grande 2010) notion of cosmopolitan modernity moves on a little from reflexive modernity as espoused in his risk society thesis. He argues that cosmopolitan modernity is part of second modernity. Like modernization or globalization, cosmopolitanism is a social process occurring inexorably worldwide. It involves the blurring of boundaries between nation-states and the influence of global processes on nation-states' politics. Increased travel across the world, the movement of workers from one country to another, the dispersion of families across the world, terrorism, biomedical tourism, the global financial crisis and the use of computerized communication technologies such as the internet have contributed to the contemporary notion of the 'global citizen' who is not simply attached to one country but sees herself or himself as transnational.

According to Beck, the pressing questions aroused by cosmopolitanism include how human rights can be preserved within a broader context of politics and what kinds of institutions and policies should be constructed to do so. Global risks generate a 'kind of "compulsory cosmopolitanism", a "glue" for diversity and plurality in a world whose boundaries are as porous as Swiss cheese' (Beck 2009b: 4). They generate new kinds of 'risk communities' which by necessity traverse nation-state boundaries. States are forced to cooperate with and help each other to deal with global risks. Awareness of the globalized nature of risks, he argues, therefore contributes to an understanding of the Other (strangers, foreigners and outsiders) and instigates an ethical position that transcends nationalities and geographical borders. These ideas build upon those earlier formulated in *Risk Society* (1992b), where Beck claimed that the globalized and therefore 'democratic' nature of risks was such that the propensity to identify the Other as the source of danger was receding.

Beck's writings on cosmopolitanism, with its emphasis on Self and Other relations, appear to draw upon Mary Douglas' work, although he mentions her only in passing. In these writings Beck is pondering the potentially positive nature of global risk society in the cosmopolitan viewpoint it encourages (or enforces). This viewpoint ideally brings groups and individuals together in a shared aim – to deal with risks – that otherwise would be suspicious of or hostile towards each other. This is largely a hopeful programme for the future, as Beck (2012) acknowledges. Beck (2011) identifies the possibility of the Self/Other distinction breaking down into a third culture of the world that incorporates both. To illustrate this he uses the example of human organ trading, where organs taken from people living in poor countries are paid for and transplanted into the bodies of wealthy Westerners, thus literally incorporating the body of the Other into the Self. Another example is surrogate motherhood undertaken by Indian women for First World couples, which involves the woman gestating a foetus from genetic material supplied by the couple and then giving them the infant after birth. Beck notes that as a result of this 'impure' cosmopolitanism, when the Other is both literally and symbolically incorporated into the boundaries of the Self, risk communities might potentially arise which are aware of the unbounded nature of risk in space and time.

> In world risk society, therefore, we experience a 'cosmopolitan imperative': There is no other any more! The global other is in our midst. Everybody is connected and confronted with everybody – even if global risks afflict different countries, states, and cultures very differently.
>
> (Beck 2011: 1348)

Cosmopolitanism brings with it a dark side, however: it is not simply about the Other being welcomed into the Self.

Beck further notes (Beck and Grande, 2010) that cosmo-politanization contains within it contradictory forces. The cosmopolitan dialectic involves the bringing together of nations as they realize their common participation in world risk society but also the tensions that underpin local resistances to globalization. The world is both brought together and torn apart by global risks. The understanding and empathy gendered by the incorporation of the Other into the Self may be somewhat fragile and dependent on economic conditions. For example, transnational labour movements cause hostility towards the foreign Other because they are seen to compete for employment with local workers (Beck 2012).

GIDDENS' PERSPECTIVES ON RISK

Anthony Giddens, in his books *The Consequences of Modernity* (1990) and *Modernity and Self-Identity* (1991), and with Lash and Beck in *Reflexive Modernization* (1994), has also written at length on risk and the uncertainty with which individuals approach life in contemporary Western societies. Like Beck, Giddens sees this uncertainty as spring-ing from the realization that the claims of modernity for human progress have been shown to be not as utopian as once was thought. Giddens' writings on risk build on his previous arguments on modernization and globalization and their relationship to the nature of everyday life. He argues that: 'One of the distinctive features of modernity, in fact, is an increasing interconnection between the two "extremes" of extensionality and intentionality: globalising influences on the one hand and personal dispositions on the other'

(Giddens 1991: 1). He is particularly interested in identifying and analysing these interconnections and reflecting on their implications for social responses to risk.

Giddens agrees with Beck in seeing late industrialism or late modernity as being characterized by transformations in traditional habits and customs, having a radical effect on the conduct and meaning of everyday life. He identifies modern institutions as being central to the nature of modernity. These institutions affect everyday life and selfhood, but in turn are themselves shaped by individuals' actions. For Giddens, the key features of modernity are institutional and individual reflexivity combined with the reorganization of time and space and the expansion of disembedding mechanisms, or mechanisms which take social relations out of their specific time/space contexts and apply them in wider locales. One of these disembedding mechanisms is systems of expert knowledge, because they deploy 'modes of technical knowledge which have validity independent of the practitioners and clients who make use of them' (Giddens 1991: 18). Other disembedding mechanisms include global standardized time zones and symbolic tokens, or objects which are media of exchange that have standard value, such as money as it is used in the global economy.

According to Giddens, in pre-modern times, space and place largely coincided, dominated by localized activities. The conditions of modernity increasingly removed space from place by fostering relationships between 'absent' others who were distant from each other. Unlike in the pre-modern era, when experiences and traditions were very much confined to particular localities and were therefore highly contextual and fragmented, late modernity brings together human experiences and knowledges. Modern institutions are unifying, establishing a 'single world', a sense of a 'we' as humanity facing problems and opportunities together which never existed in pre-modernity (Giddens 1991: 27). This approach is very similar to Beck's concepts of 'world risk society' and 'cosmopolitanism'.

Giddens (1990: 10) refers to the 'double-edged character of modernity', or the risks associated with the drive for progress. Because of disembedding mechanisms and globalization, events now may have potentially disastrous effects that are far more wide-reaching than previously. The fall of the global capitalist economy affects the life chances of millions; a malfunction in a nuclear power plant equally may kill or harm millions. Giddens describes late modernity, therefore, as 'a risk culture' (1991: 3). He emphasizes that he does not mean by this term that people in contemporary Western societies are more exposed to danger or are more anxious about threats to their welfare than they were earlier. In previous eras, there were fears of terrible catastrophes affecting the world and destroying humankind. In the present day, however, such fears are commonly linked to the perception that humans (rather than the gods or fate) have brought these catastrophes upon themselves (Giddens 1990: 121–2). The threats are therefore of a different kind, part of the 'dark side of modernity' (ibid.: 122). Hazards and dangers are now conceptualized as 'risks' rather than as givens, things over which humans are seen as potentially exerting control: 'it is a society increasingly preoccupied with the future (and also with safety) which generates the notion of risk' (Giddens 1998: 27).

Giddens therefore displays a similar position to Beck on the nature of risk in relating it to hazards or dangers that exist objectively, differ substantively from previous eras and are now linked to human responsibility. He describes the notion of risk as moving through two stages which roughly correspond to Beck's observations about changes in conceptualizing and dealing with risk in early modern and late modern eras. In the first stage, risk is seen as 'an essential calculus', a way of promoting certainty and order in the precision of risk calculations, of 'bringing the future under control', where the various components of risk are 'given' and thus able to be calculated (Giddens 1994: 58–9). It is upon this notion of risk that the welfare state developed as a means of protecting populations from the risks of actuarially calculable threats such as illness and unemployment with the use of social insurance schemes (Giddens 1998: 27–8). The second stage is where we are not able to precisely calculate risk, but rather develop 'scenarios' of risk with various degrees of plausibility. One example is global warming, subject to expert dispute over whether or not it is happening and how serious its ramifications are. As an outcome of modernity, there are now far greater uncertainties than ever previously existed.

Like Beck, Giddens describes modern reflexivity as being different from the reflexive monitoring which has always been part of human activity. Modern reflexivity, for both individuals and institutions, involves awareness of the contingent nature of expert knowledges and social activity, their susceptibility to revision and change (Giddens 1991: 20). This reflexivity is both the product of the Enlightenment and confounds its expectations of inexorable human progress through knowledge. The conditions of modernity – the progressive separation of space, place and time and the increasing role played by disembedding mechanisms – all depend upon trust, vested not in individuals but in 'abstract capacities' (Giddens 1990: 26). People now cannot simply rely on local knowledges, tradition, religious precepts, habit or observation of others' practices to conduct their everyday lives, as they did in pre-modern and early modern times. Rather, they must look principally to experts they do not personally know and are unlikely ever to meet to supply them with guidelines.

Modernity is also characterized by doubt about the validity of knowledges, acknowledging that all knowledge is open to revision. Greater knowledge had led in turn to greater uncertainty: 'The fact that experts frequently disagree becomes familiar terrain for almost everyone' (Giddens 1994: 186). The reflexive organization of knowledge environments requires the constant prediction of the nature of outcomes in the future, or risk assessment. This assessment, by its very nature, is always imprecise, for these calculations rely upon abstract knowledge systems which are subject to contestation and change. As a result, people have become increasingly cynical about the claims to progress offered by traditional modernity: hence the continual reflexivity of individuals and institutions. In pre-modern eras, reflexivity was largely structured by the traditions established within the time–space organization of individual communities. In modernity, reflexivity took on a different character – tradition became less important as a justification for action. Instead, 'social practices are constantly examined and reformed in the light of incoming information about those very practices, thus constitutively altering their character' (Giddens 1990: 38).

Giddens (1990: 111) argues that the concept of risk is antithetical to that of fate, because fate assumes a predestined path. While notions of fate and destiny may still exist in late modernity, that of risk is also dominant. Risk assumes that there are no aspects of human action that follow a preordained course, but rather they are open to contingencies: 'Living in a "risk society" means living with a calculative attitude to the open possibilities of action, positive and negative, with which, as individuals and globally, we are confronted in a continuous way in our contemporary social existence' (Giddens 1991: 28). Risk assessment involves weighing up and choosing among various possible courses of action according to their predicted outcomes. Modernity, therefore, is oriented towards the future, while pre-modernity was oriented to the past (ibid.: 29).

Because the self is seen as a reflexive project in late modernity, as a problematic rather than a given, there is far more emphasis on the malleability of the self and the responsibility that one takes for one's life trajectory. Individuals have greater recourse to expert knowledges in constructing the project of the self (Giddens 1991: 32–3). As knowledge is being constantly revised in late modernity, the processes of reflexivity are more complicated and uncertain. There are more choices to be made. Because traditions have lost their power and there is more 'openness' about how one can live, the concept of lifestyle has become ever more important to selfhood, forcing people to negotiate among a range of options. The reflexive project of self-identity requires 'consideration of risks as filtered through contact with expert knowledge' (ibid.: 5). So too, Giddens argues, the body is seen less and less as a 'given' but rather as subject to individual manipulation and will: it is, therefore, 'reflexively mobilized' (ibid.: 7). Developments in the fields of science and medicine contribute to the notion that the body is amenable to human action, such as reproductive technologies, genetic engineering and surgical procedures. Here Giddens' writings again closely parallel those of Beck, this time in relation to the processes that Beck calls 'individualization'.

In his most recent writings, Giddens, like Beck, has turned his attention to globalization (Giddens 2003, 2005) and the politics of climate change (Giddens 2011). Again like Beck, Giddens (2003) refers to a global cosmopolitan society, but he is somewhat more pessimistic about the possibilities of globalization than is Beck. Giddens cautions that risks are associated with this new society. He draws a distinction between 'cosmopolitans' who welcome the changes and intersections wrought by the forces of globalization, and 'fundamentalists', who resist change, finding it disturbing and dangerous. Fundamentalists seek to preserve the boundaries between nation-states, ethnicities or between different religions and ways of life, and have resorted to political demonstrations, violence, discourses of hatred and terrorism to do so.

In his focus on the hazards produced by globalization, Giddens (2005: 22) defines risk as a phenomenon coming into prominence in societies that are 'future-oriented', actively attempting to break away from their past ways of life. He refers to the family as the site of major upheaval and the production of risks as a result of detraditionalization and the responses of fundamentalism. He notes that intense debates have emerged in most countries about gender equality, the regulation of sexuality and the role of the family.

Fundamentalism has again emerged in response to conservative views about the importance of maintaining tradition. One area is which this has been evident is the debate about gay marriage in Anglophone countries, where the concept of 'marriage' has been held up to examination. Traditionalists (or fundamentalists in their most extreme form) have insisted that marriage should only be a formal union between a man and a woman and that any moves to legalize and formalize marriage between gay couples poses a threat to conventional marriage and the concept of 'the family'.

Fundamentalists have developed transnational groups to fight for the preservation of tradition. Nation-states therefore mostly no longer have specific enemies as such, but rather face risks and dangers from groups allied across national boundaries. Giddens (2005) refers to the 'new-style terrorist' groups such as al-Qaeda that have benefitted from globalization in being able to finance their activities globally and communicate, organize and construct weapons via globalized systems of mass transportation and digital media. Their goals are not local, as in the old-style terrorist groups such as the IRA, but dispersed and far-reaching. The 11 September 2001 terrorist attack on the United States is one of the most well-known examples of new-style fundamentalists' attempts to preserve tradition. Giddens (2005) penned a prescient warning, published in January 2005, that Britain very likely faced an imminent terrorist attack from religious fundamentalists. Six months later this attack occurred in the 7 July London bombings.

In *The Politics of Climate Change* (2011) Giddens looks at the debates between climate change believers and sceptics and the different ways in which the risks related to climate change are positioned from these two opposing camps. From the position of a supporter of the dominant thesis of those who argue that humans have caused climate change, he ponders the question why it is so difficult for lay people and governments to recognize the pressing risks posed by climate change and take action to avert these risks. Giddens (2011) uses the term 'the Giddens paradox' to describe the phenomenon by which people tend not to become concerned about the dangers already caused by climate change because they are not immediate, tangible or obvious. The paradox is that if nothing is done to deal with these dangers, then they will become worse and less reversible.

RISK AND TRUST

One difference between Beck and Giddens is that in the latter's writings on risk and late modernity, the notion of trust is dominant. Giddens asserts that with the late modern reliance on generalized expert systems over local knowledges, and upon symbolic tokens such as money, trust remains a necessary part of life: 'The disembedded characteristics of abstract systems mean constant interaction with "absent others" – people one never sees or meets but whose actions directly affect features of one's own life' (Giddens 1994: 89). However, if expert knowledges fail, the repercussions extend far beyond the local context. Reliance upon global expert systems, therefore, is characterized by uncertainty. People are required to be more challenging of expert knowledges, requiring of them that they win their trust. They are also turning back towards face-to-face relationships in the attempt to 're-embed' their trust in those whom they know personally.

This involves different sorts of trust relations, based on intimate others, and different sorts of risks. In the case of both experts and intimate others, trust must be won and continually negotiated.

Trust presupposes awareness of risk, offering reliability in the face of contingent outcomes and thereby serving to minimize concern about possible risk (Giddens 1990: 35). Trust is vital to establish ontological security from infancy onwards. Giddens defines ontological security as an emotional phenomenon, incorporating 'the confidence that most human beings have in the continuity of their self-identity and in the constancy of the surrounding social and material environments of action' (ibid.: 92). It incorporates trust in the reliability of persons and things. Trust, therefore, may be regarded as a means of dealing psychologically with risks that would otherwise paralyze action or lead to feelings of engulfment, dread and anxiety. Without trust, people could not engage in the 'leap of faith' that is required of them in dealing with these expert knowledge systems of which they themselves have little understanding or technical knowledge because they have not been trained in them.

Trust may result from reflexive calculation or else simply from choosing to invest faith in an individual or organization. It allows individuals to develop a cocoon of invulnerability which enables them to get on with life, to fend off their knowledge of the risks that await them at every turn. This protective cocoon is sometimes pierced by experiences that highlight the existence of these risks and call into question established routines. Giddens calls these experiences 'fateful moments' (1991:40), which must be dealt with by reference to moral or existential criteria. Sometimes people may deliberately seek out these risks (see discussion of this in Chapter 8). But it is often the case that the cocoon is re-established, allowing the sense of relative invulnerability to return and thus fending off dread and anxiety (ibid.: 40). Everyday routines are also vital to the establishment and maintenance of ontological security, allowing people to habitually deal with dangers and associated fears.

Notions of fate tend to re-enter in the face of low-probability but high-consequence risks over which individuals have no personal control. Sometimes the differences between expert knowledges will be so great that the individual is forced to rely on fate, to take a chance. Deciding simply to trust in abstract systems or to decide that fate will take its own course regardless – what Giddens terms 'pragmatic acceptance' – ostensibly relieves the burden of anxiety (1990: 133). However, he claims that as a result, anxieties are simply pushed deeper into the unconscious. Fear is therefore not dispelled, but rather displaced, for the possibility of disaster is still there. Other reactions to risk are 'sustained optimism', or holding onto Enlightenment faith in providential reason; 'cynical pessimism', or dampening the emotional impact of anxieties by approaching them with a humorous or world-weary per-spective; and 'radical engagement', or an attitude of practical contestation towards perceived sources of danger, such as is found in the new social movements such as the green movement (ibid.: 135–7).

Like Beck, Giddens has also published on love and sexual relationships in his book *The Transformation of Intimacy* (1992), where he discusses the risks associated with 'opening' oneself to another and seeking the 'pure' relationship. Giddens argues that people have become dependent on a very small number of personal relationships, particularly those involving romantic love and marriage, to find a sense of security and to construct subjectivity. He claims that there is a high level of anxiety and lack of certainty around love relationships in a social world of changing gender and family roles, characterized by a tension between retaining a sense of autonomy as an individual and a need for close relationships with others.

Giddens introduced his notion of the 'pure relationship' in *Modernity and Self-Identity*, arguing that it is 'one in which external criteria have become dissolved: the relationship exists solely for whatever rewards that relationship as such can deliver' (1991: 6). Trust plays a role in the pure relationship, mobilized through joint disclosure of personal thoughts and feelings rather than being anchored in criteria outside the relationship itself, such as social duty or traditional obligation. The 'pure relationship', therefore, is also highly reflexive, requiring constant work to maintain it. It presupposes 'commitment', but this commitment must be actively won and negotiated, based on intimacy. The sphere of personal relationships is seen to be a place where intimacy may be established, bolstering one against the uncertainties of the external world. Yet personal relationships and intimacy are themselves dogged by risks, because of the greater 'openness' and breakdown of traditional norms. There is far more scope for variation in intimate relationships such as marriages and other close love relationships, such as those between same-sex partners and between parents and children (ibid.: 12).

Trust at the personal level is a project to be worked at, demanding that each party 'open out' to the other, in the absence of fixed codes (Giddens 1990: 121). Giddens attributes our obsession with the quality of relationships as resulting from this need to work on trust: erotic involvement particularly calls for self-disclosure. To know the other, one must know oneself (ibid.: 122). The trust that one invests in an intimate other can be severed at any time: through a broken love affair, the intimate other becomes a stranger. The 'opening up' of oneself to another, therefore, is characterized by ambivalence, anxiety and risk. As a result, intimate relationships are the site of profound insecurity at the same time as they hold out the promise of ontological security.

CONCLUDING COMMENTS

As I have shown in this chapter, there are major convergences between Beck's and Giddens' theorizing on risk in the context of late modernity. Both see the concept of risk as a central concern in the contemporary era, emerging from the processes of modernization. Risks are seen to have changed in their character in late modern society, having greater ramifications in their impact across space and time. Both Beck and Giddens are interested in the political aspects of risk, singling out reflexivity as a primary response to uncertainty and insecurity in late modernity. They identify a greater awareness on the part of lay people that the claims of 'experts' about risk are often uncertain or clash with each other, and a willingness on lay people's part to challenge experts, governments and industry in relation to risk concerns. Beck and Giddens extend their discussion of reflexivity into the realm of private life and intimate relationships, remarking upon the ways in which risk and its associated reflexivity have permeated this realm. Both Beck and Giddens take a weak social constructionist (critical realist) approach to risk and share an approach which is founded in critical structuralism, in focusing their attention on how risk is generated and dealt with at the macro-structural level of society, the political implications of this and the social conflicts that arise.

There are also a number of important differences between the two theorists' takes on risk. One is the relationship that is implied between risk and reflexivity to risk. Beck implies that a heightened degree of risk reflexivity is the outcome of a greater number of risks being produced in the late modern era. Giddens sees the relationship as being the other way round. Risks are not greater in number in late modernity. It is simply that they are *thought* to be greater, because the nature of subjectivity in general has changed to an approach to life that is far more sensitive to the possibility of risk than in previous eras. Further, Beck and Giddens represent expert knowledge systems in different ways. For Giddens, reflexivity takes place through expert systems and is reliant upon lay people's trust in expertise. For Beck, reflexivity is a critique of expertise, based not in trust but in distrust of expert systems, particularly in relation to environmental hazards. Giddens also focuses more on self-reflexivity, reflexivity directed towards the body and the self, than does Beck, who places greater emphasis on individuals' reflexive critique of the social conflicts and thus is more challenging of current social arrangements than is Giddens (Lash 1994: 116; Lash and Urry 1994: 38).

Some major criticisms of the assertions of Beck and Giddens have been advanced. Beck has a stylistic habit of making bold sweeping, generalizing statements which, if analysed closely, often do not bear up under the weight of close examination. His prolific writings, many of which tend to repeat the same general statements, also sometimes contradict each other in their detail. As a result, his body of work on risk has been subject to quite intense and detailed criticism by other sociologists. Mythen (2007: 799–801) summarizes several criticisms of Beck put forward by a number of scholars. These include the claim that Beck's distinction between 'natural hazards' and 'manufactured risks' overlooks the continuing effects of 'natural' catastrophes such as floods and earthquakes in the contemporary world and fails to recognize that human-made hazards have a much longer history than allowed in his thesis. Further, the distinction he makes between 'natural' and 'manufactured' hazards positions an artificial distinction between the two, when they should be seen instead as interrelated. Thus, for example, the 'natural' event of flooding is influenced by the processes of modernization. Critics have also pointed out that rather than risk being 'democratized' and spread equally over social groups and nations, the disadvantaged and marginalized still are affected to a greater extent than are socio-economically advantaged groups and nations. Beck has also been criticized for over-stating and over-generalizing the severity of risks in the global context, without acknowledging that in many countries life expectancy and morbidity from disease have vastly improved in the late modern era.

Both Beck and Giddens argue that the reflexive critique of science and other expert knowledge systems, as well as social movements, are features solely of late modernity, and were not found in earlier modernity. Some commentators have argued that this is not the case, and that Beck's and Giddens' representations of modernity are simplistic, not acknowledging the complexity of responses to expert knowledges. Lash (1993: 5) asserts, for example, that modernity is by definition reflexive, involving continual monitoring of itself, even if through convention rather than through individualization. Other criticisms put forward are that Beck and Giddens are too speculative, making broad and loose speculations about structural and organizational processes, without grounding these specifically enough in the actual processes and experiences of institutional and everyday life. Beck's lack of attention to the everyday experiences of risk as part of ordinary routines and his general failure to differentiate between different genders, nationalities, socio-economic status and so on, are other features of his work that other risk scholars find problematic (Tulloch and Lupton 2003; Hannah-Moffat and O'Malley 2007). Further, it may be argued that Beck and Giddens do not sufficiently acknowledge the communal, aesthetic and shared symbolic aspects of risk in their focus on individualization (Lash 1993, 1994, 2000; Alexander 1996; see also the discussion in Chapter 6).

Beck's later work on cosmopolitanism and world risk society contains many of the same deficiencies, particularly his over-generalizing and tendency towards sweeping statements without acknowledging the situated nature of risk experiences and perceptions. Critics have further asserted that speaking of a 'risk society' or 'world risk society' is reductive and totalizing in focusing on risk to the exclusion of other issues (Rasborg 2012), and that Beck's approach to cosmopolitanism glosses over inequalities and injustices globally and is rather naïve in its hopeful approach to mutual cooperation (Martell 2009).

As for Giddens' recent work on risk, his writings on the politics of climate change have come in for particular criticism. It has been argued that few of his contentions in the book are new, that his argument is simplistic and that he has not acknowledged previous scholarship in the area. Critics are particularly scathing about the fact that he named the 'Giddens paradox' after himself, especially given that this paradox has been observed and commented upon by many others prior to Giddens writing about it (see, for example, a review of the first edition of *The Politics of Climate Change* by Castree 2010).

Despite these criticisms, Beck's and Giddens' speculations on the nature of risk in contemporary societies have been enormously influential in Anglophone sociology, more so than any of the other sociocultural perspectives discussed in this book. This is not surprising, for their insights into the structural and political features of risk, the changes in the meanings of risk over the eras of pre-modernity, early modernity and late modernity and the implications of current ideas about risk for subjectivity and social relations in many ways are valuable and suggestive.

5

RISK AND GOVERNMENTALITY

In Chapter 4, the views on risk as a product of late modernity put forward by Beck and Giddens were discussed. Those who have taken up a perspective on risk drawing on the writings of Michel Foucault are also interested in the ways in which risk operates in late modernity, particularly in relation to the political ethos of neo-liberalism, which currently dominates in Anglophone countries. They similarly see the intensification of discussions of risk and risk practices as an outcome of the social changes occurring in the wake of modernization.

One major difference between the two perspectives is that while the 'risk society' approach tends to take a weak social constructionist or critical realist stance on risk in concert with a critical structuralist perspective, advocates of Foucauldian approaches mostly adopt a 'strong' version of social constructionism and a poststructuralist approach to power relations. The concept of discourse, as noted in Chapter 2, is integral to Foucauldian theorizing. An important insight offered by Foucauldian perspectives on risk is the ways in which the discourses, strategies, practices and institutions around a phenomenon such as risk serve to bring it into being, to construct it as a phenomenon. It is argued that it is only through these discourses, strategies, practices and institutions that we come to know 'risk'. They produce 'truths' on risk that are then the basis for action. For Foucauldian writers, therefore, the nature of risk itself is not the important question for analysis. Risk is seen as a 'calculative rationality' rather than as a thing in itself (Dean 1999).

This chapter looks at the ways in which the discourses, knowledges, strategies, practices and institutions that have developed around risk both reflect and construct a distinct approach to selfhood, society and the government of populations. It begins with a discussion of the relationship between governmentality and risk, and goes on to explore the movement from the concept of 'dangerousness' to that of 'risk' in medical, legal and social welfare discourses. Then follows a discussion of three types of contemporary risk rationalities: (1) insurantial risk; (2) epidemiological risk; and (3) case-management or clinical risk. The chapter ends with an account of the most recent perspective on risk offered by governmentality scholars: that of precautionary risk, an approach developed in response to the new global catastrophes of the twenty-first century.

GOVERNMENTALITY

Michel Foucault himself did not dwell specifically on the topic of risk in his writings at any great length. However, much of what he had to say on governmentality and modernity has been considered relevant by a number of scholars who have applied some of his ideas to the analysis of risk as a sociocultural phenomenon. Governmentality is the approach to social regulation and control that, according to Foucault (1991), began to emerge in the sixteenth century in Europe, associated with such social changes as the breakdown in the feudal system and the development of administrative states in its place, based on the principles of legitimate rule. By the eighteenth century, the early modern European states began to think of their citizens in terms of populations, or 'society', a social body requiring intervention, management and protection so as to maximize wealth, welfare and productivity. Such features of populations as demographic estimates, marriage and fertility statistics, life expectation tables and mortality rates became central to the project of a technology of population. The body of both the individual and that of populations became the bearer of new variables. These variables included not only those between the healthy and the sick, the strong and the weak, the rich and the poor, and so on, but between the more or less utilizable, more or less amenable to profitable investment, those with greater or lesser prospects of illness or death and with more or less capacity for being usefully trained (Foucault 1984: 278–9).

Governmentality as a strategy and rationale, Foucault claims, has dominated political power in Western countries since the eighteenth century. In its contemporary form it is characterized by an approach to political rule, neo-liberalism, which champions individual freedom and rights against the excessive intervention of the state. The domain of government is extensive, focusing on the complex of humans interactions with a diversity of phenomena:

> The things with which in this sense government is to be concerned are in fact men [sic], but men in their relations,

their links, their imbrication with those other things which are wealth, resources, means of subsistence, the territory with its specific qualities, climate, irrigation, fertility, etc.; men in their relation to that other kind of things, customs, habits, ways of acting and thinking, etc.; lastly, men in their relation to that other kind of things, accidents and misfortunes such as famine, epidemics, death, etc.

(Foucault 1991: 93)

Foucault, like Beck and Giddens, emphasizes the role of expert knowledges in the constitution of late modern subjectivity. Expert knowledges, he argues, are integral to the reflexive techniques and practices of subjectification, or the formation of certain types of subject. For Foucault, however, expert knowledges are not transparently a means to engage in reflexivity. Rather, they are seen as pivotal to governmentality, providing the guidelines and advice by which populations are surveyed, compared against norms, trained to conform to these norms and rendered productive. Central to these technologies is normalization, or the method by which norms of behaviour or health status are identified in populations and sub-groups of populations. Through normalization, the late modern individual is fabricated within a network of instruments and techniques of power. The technologies of mass surveillance, monitoring, observation and measurement are central to this disciplinary power, helping to construct understandings of bodies in space and time and to use these understandings to regulate them.

From this perspective, risk may be understood as a governmental strategy of regulatory power by which populations and individuals are monitored and managed through the goals of neo-liberalism. Risk is governed via a heterogeneous network of interactive actors, institutions, knowledges and practices. Information about diverse risks is collected and analysed by medical researchers, statisticians, sociologists, demographers, environmental scientists, legal practitioners, statisticians, bankers and accountants, to name but a few. Through these never-ceasing efforts, risk is problematized, rendered calculable and governable. So too, through these efforts, particular social groups or populations are identified as 'at risk' or 'high risk', requiring particular forms of knowledges and interventions. Indeed, one could refer to 'risk assemblages', which are configured using the data derived from surveillance technologies and managed by a diverse range of agencies and from a range of sites. For example, Rich *et al.* (2011) have conducted an analysis of the ways in which schoolchildren's bodies are monitored and regulated via surveillance techniques in the context of the 'obesity epidemic'. They note that risk assemblages of schoolchildren's bodies in the UK are constantly configured and reconfigured with the use of such technologies as biometric fingerprint screening to record, monitor and regulate school lunch choices; pedometers to measure the number of steps children take; skinfold measurements to monitor body fat; heart rate monitors; measurement of height and weight to construct a BMI; and lunch box inspections. These technologies combine to collate data on children's bodies which is constantly subject to revision and therefore to change. Such technologies are central to contemporary processes of normalization, configuring a risk assemblage that is compared against documented norms and either found to be acceptable ('normal') or at-risk ('overweight' or 'obese') and therefore requiring intervention and further monitoring.

Risk, from the Foucauldian perspective, is 'a moral technology. To calculate a risk is to master time, to discipline the future' (Ewald 1991: 207). For some scholars drawing upon Foucault's writings, risk is viewed as a 'dispositif', a term used to encompass the governing of social problems, configuring a heterogeneous assemblage of discursive, administrative, technical, legal, institutional and material elements (Aradau and van Muster 2007: 91). A dispositif relates to the bringing together of these heterogeneous elements as part of the exercise of power and refers to the system of relations between these elements. A dispositif of risk 'creates a specific relation to the future, which requires the monitoring of the future, the attempt to calculate what the future can offer and the necessity to control and minimize its potentially harmful effects' (ibid.: 97–8).

The risk dispositifs of governmentality, expressed in the neo-liberal states that emerged in the West in late modernity, include both direct, coercive strategies to regulate populations, but also, and most importantly, less direct strategies that rely on individuals' voluntary compliance with the interests and needs of the state. These strategies are diverse and multi-centred, emerging not only from the state but also other agencies and institutions, such as the mass media. A crucial aspect of governmentality as it is expressed in neo-liberal states is that the regulation and disciplining of citizens are directed at the autonomous, self-regulated individual. Rather than a sovereign state seeking to impose power from above by using overtly directive, punitive or constraining means of disciplining its subjects and maintaining social order, neo-liberal governance relies on productive and dispersed forms of authority. Citizens are cultivated to govern themselves and to focus on self-actualization rather than emancipation. Citizens are positioned in governmental discourses, therefore, as active rather than passive subjects of governance. Rather than mainly being externally policed by agents of the state, individuals police themselves, they exercise power upon themselves as normalized subjects who are in pursuit of their own best interests and freedom, who are interested in self-improvement, seeking happiness and healthiness (Gordon 1991; Dean 2007, 2010).

As will be explained in greater detail below, the concept of risk, as it is developed through normalization, initially deflects attention away from individuals and their behaviours towards aggregates or populations. The information gathered about risk from population data, however, is then often employed in advice to individuals about how they should conduct their lives. Discourses on risk are directed at the regulation of the body: how it moves in space, how it interacts with other bodies and things. These discourses also contribute to the constitution of selfhood, or subjectivity, and thus are part of the panoply of 'practices' or 'technologies of the self' (Foucault 1988). Through the technologies of the self, the individual becomes the 'entrepreneur of himself or herself in terms of attempting to maximize her or his "human capital"' (Gordon 1991: 44). People attempt to 'transform themselves in order to attain a certain state of happiness, purity, wisdom, perfection, or immortality' (Foucault 1988: 18). In doing so, they seek out and adopt advice from institutional governmental agencies, from experts who have problematized areas of life as pervaded by risk. As expert knowledge about risk has proliferated in late modernity, the various strategies which individuals are required to practise upon themselves to avoid risk have equally proliferated.

Consider the example of the pregnant woman in the contemporary era. More so than in previous eras because of the growth of risk-related knowledges and technologies surrounding pregnancy, this woman is surrounded by, and constructed through, a plethora of expert and lay advice. This advice is directed at how she should regulate her body with its precious cargo, the foetus, which is portrayed as being highly fragile and susceptible to risk at every stage of its development. Even from the time a woman may be considering the idea of child-bearing, she is exhorted to engage in certain practices to ensure that fertilization will take place successfully and that her body is at its peak state of health. She is encouraged to read as much as possible about pregnancy and childbirth, so that she knows what to expect and which risks she should avoid. She is told to avoid smoking, drinking alcohol and coffee and taking other drugs, to eat a nutritious diet and engage in regular exercise.

Once pregnant, these strategies and more must be adhered to by the woman. The pregnant woman must be highly careful of any food she eats, avoiding a range of foods that may contain listeria bacteria or toxoplasmosis protozoa, both of which may cause miscarriage or birth defects. She is advised to closely monitor her body for signs of an ectopic pregnancy or miscarriage, such as abdominal cramps or vaginal bleeding. She should not take any medicines, unless she has first checked their safety for the foetus with her doctor. She is encouraged to regularly see a doctor for ante-natal checks, including a series of blood tests and such tests as ultrasound and, in some cases, amniocentesis (testing of the genetic make-up of the foetus) to monitor the health and normality of the foetus. She is encouraged to attend ante-natal classes to prepare for childbirth.

Many of the discourses of risk that surround the pregnant woman suggest that it is her responsibility to ensure the health of her foetus, and that if she were to ignore expert advice, she is culpable should her baby miscarry or be born with a defect. The pregnant woman, therefore, is positioned as a risk assemblage in a web of surveillance, monitoring, measurement and expert advice that requires constant work on her part: seeking out knowledge about risks to her foetus, acting according to that knowledge. Yet the discourses of risk that surround her are generally embraced willingly, because the woman herself wants to maximize the health of her foetus, to achieve the 'perfect child'. Although some women in some countries such as the United States have been prosecuted and imprisoned for 'foetal endangerment' by refusing to take medical advice or give up using certain drugs, most women are not coerced through overt disciplinary means to accede to expert advice. No-one forces them to buy books on pregnancy, to watch their diet, give up alcohol, and attend ante-natal checks and classes. Because pregnant women have been discursively positioned within a context in which the general consensus is that foetuses are precious and fragile and that it is up to the pregnant woman to protect them, and that infants are very important individuals who deserve the best start in life, most women voluntarily engage in such risk-avoidance strategies, accepting the responsibility implied.

To resist these strategies is difficult, for it is tantamount to declaring that the woman does not care about her own health and welfare, and more importantly, that of the foetus she is carrying and is expected to protect and nourish in the proper maternal manner. Indeed, she may actively demand greater access to medical surveillance, such as numerous ultrasounds, in the attempt to alleviate her anxieties and concerns about her foetus and the risks to which it is exposed. The technologies of selfhood and embodiment in relation to pregnancy demonstrate the intersection and alignment of institutional and experts' objectives in advising and regulating the pregnant woman principally through directives intended for her to police herself, and the woman's own concerns to take such advice (see Lupton 2012b, for further discussion of these points).

In late modern societies, not to engage in risk-avoiding behaviour is considered 'a failure of the self to take care of itself – a form of irrationality, or simply a lack of skilfulness' (Greco 1993: 361). Risk-avoiding behaviour, therefore, becomes viewed as a moral enterprise relating to issues of self-control, self-knowledge and self-improvement. It is a form of self-government, involving the acceptance and internalization of the objectives of institutional government. Because the project of selfhood is never complete, but rather is continuing throughout the lifespan, so too the project of risk avoidance as a technology of the self is never-ending, requiring eternal vigilance.

FROM DANGEROUSNESS TO RISK

Several commentators adopting the governmentality approach have observed that the concept of 'dangerousness' has been replaced by that of 'risk' in institutions' dealings with marginalized social groups and individuals. In nineteenth-century governmental discourses, as part of the emergent new ways of thinking about the citizen, the concept of 'dangerousness' tended to be used in relation to the problems of health and crime. 'Dangerous classes' and the 'dangerous individual' were identified as possessing the inherent qualities to present a danger to themselves or to others, and therefore as prime targets for governmental intervention and treatment. The notion of 'dangerousness' was derived from expert judgements on such features as the state of living conditions and moral climate in which social groups dwelt. Members of the working class and the poor were typically constituted as dangerous. Against these dangerous classes were juxtaposed their antithesis: those (generally more socially and economically privileged) classes who were seen to be 'at risk' from the depravations or contamination of members of the dangerous classes (Kendall and Wickham 1992: 11–12).

Castel (1991) links the concept of risk with that of governmentality by focusing on contemporary preventive strategies of social administration in the United States and France. He argues that these strategies are innovative in that they 'dissolve the notion of a *subject* or a concrete individual, and put in its place a combination of *factors*, the factors of risk' (ibid.: 281, original emphases). As a result, he argues, there have been changes in the ways in which intervention is carried out. No longer is the essential component of intervention

the direct face-to-face relationship between the carer and the cared, the helper and the helped, the professional and the client. It comes instead to reside in the establishing

> of flows of population based on the collation of a range of
> abstract factors deemed liable to produce risk in general.
>
> (Castel 1991: 281)

Specialist professionals are cast in a more subordinate role, while managerial policy formations take over.

In psychiatric medicine, for example, there has been a shift over the past century from the use of the notion of 'dangerousness' used in relation to people with psychiatric disorders to that of 'risk'. In classical psychiatry, '"risk" meant essentially the danger embodied in the mentally ill person capable of violent and unpredictable action' (Castel 1991: 283). Dangerousness itself connoted an immanent quality of the subject, a potentiality that dwelt within and may or may not have been manifested. Therefore there could only ever be imputations of dangerousness, based on observation of a patient's present symptoms and speculations about what these might mean for future behaviour. All insane people were deemed as carrying this potentiality for dangerousness within them, despite their otherwise benign exteriors, and were subsequently treated with such preventive strategies as confinement from the rest of the society (ibid.).

In contrast, the notion of risk, although also acknowledging potentiality, is calculated through systematic statistical correlations and probabilities based on populations rather than the close observation of individuals. Risk is therefore more selective and precise, but at the same time applies to a larger group of people than the notion of dangerousness:

> A risk does not arise from the presence of particular precise
> danger embodied in a concrete individual or group. It is the

effect of a combination of abstract *factors* which render more or less probable the occurrence of undesirable modes of behaviour.

(Castel 1991: 287, original emphasis)

To be designated 'at risk' is to be located within a network of factors drawn from the observation of others, to be designated as part of a 'risk population'. A risk, therefore, is one step further from dangerousness in its potentiality.

Identifying and monitoring risks in populations constitute 'a new mode of surveillance: that of systematic predetection' (Castel 1991: 288). This new form of surveillance may not necessarily require the actual presence of the 'risky' individual, but may be based on the monitoring of records:

To intervene no longer means, or at least not to begin with, taking as one's target a given individual, in order to correct, punish or care for him or her ... There is, in fact, no longer a relation of immediacy with a subject *because there is no longer a subject*. What the new preventive policies primarily address is no longer individuals but factors, statistical correlations of heterogeneous elements. They deconstruct the concrete subject of intervention, and reconstruct a combination of factors liable to produce risk. Their primary aim is not to confront a concrete dangerous situation, but to anticipate all the possible forms of irruption of danger.

(Castel 1991: 288, original emphasis)

Under this new approach to surveillance, for a person to be identified as posing a risk no longer means that she or he has to be individually observed for signs of dangerousness. It is enough that she or he is identified as a member of a 'risky population', based on a 'risk profile' developed from calculations using demographic and other characteristics. Castel notes that this shift from dangerousness to risk results in the production of 'a potentially infinite multiplication of the possibilities for intervention. For what situation is there of which one can be certain that it harbours no risk, no uncontrollable or unpredictable chance factor?' (1991: 289).

Whereas in the early modern era members of the 'dangerous classes' were disciplined and managed via coercive, exclusionary and correctional strategies (such as incarceration), risk-based tactics and strategies may focus very little on the individual characteristics of those identified as being 'at risk', but rather direct attention at changing the environment in which such individuals operate. One example is situational crime prevention. As a risk management strategy, situational crime prevention deals hardly at all with individual offenders. It is not interested in the causes of crime and does not support correctional strategies for managing crime (O'Malley 1992). The philosophy of this approach, as articulated in an American National Crime Prevention Institute document, is that: 'Criminal behaviour can be controlled primarily through the direct alteration of the environment of potential victims … As criminal opportunity is reduced, so too will be the number of criminals' (quoted in ibid.: 262). The focus of this approach is upon prevention of crime rather than rehabilitation of offenders.

The shift in focus in expert knowledges and practices from the concept of 'dangerousness' to 'risk' has a number of consequences. The future behaviour of a marginalized individual deemed subject to external intervention and regulation is no longer linked exclusively to that individual's own behaviour, based on close observation of her or him. Because the concept of risk has emerged, which is predicated on techniques of the surveillance and measurement of populations and statistical calculations based on data derived from these techniques, marginalized individuals are now dealt with differently. Under the discourse of risk, these people are typically categorized as a member of a specific 'risk group' and their future behaviour is gauged and the interventions that are judged to be required are based on the characteristics of this group. These calculations rest upon a notion of management that highlights the importance of rationalized and standardized assessment and prediction and a notion of the individual actor that represents her or him as behaving predictably, in alliance with patterns identified in wider populations.

CONTEMPORARY RISK STRATEGIES

The above discussion on the change from 'dangerousness' to 'risk' as a discourse and strategy of regulation and intervention tends to imply a homogeneous approach to risk in contemporary Western societies. This is not quite the case. Dean (1997, 1999) has identified three types of risk rationalities in neo-liberal societies. These include insurantial risk, epidemiological risk and case-management or clinical risk. There are certain differences between these risk rationalities, based on the types of risk calculations that are manifested and the specific risks to which they are directed.

Ewald (1991) has discussed three characteristics of the insurantial risk rationality, or that operating in the discourses and strategies of insurance. The first is that risk is distinguished from a bet in that it is seen to be calculable, governed by identifiable laws. For an event to be a risk in insurance discourses, it must be possible to evaluate the probability of it happening. The second characteristic is that risk is collective, affecting a population rather than an individual: 'Strictly speaking there is no such thing as an individual risk; otherwise insurance would be no more than a wager' (ibid.: 203). Rather, risk is seen as something that only becomes calculable when it is spread over a population. Each individual in a specified population is understood to be a factor of risk or exposed to a risk, but each individual is not equally likely to fall prey to a risk or cause the same degree of risk (ibid.: 203). The third characteristic of insurantial risk is that it is a capital. What is insured against is not the injury or loss but rather a capital against whose loss the insurer offers a guarantee. The injury or loss is not prevented or repaired, but is given a price for financial compensation.

Insurance, therefore, is a means for dealing with the vagaries of fate, a technology through which risk is constructed as a schema of rationality, of ordering elements of reality, allowing for a certain way of objectifying things, people and the relationships between them. Insurers 'produce risk' by rendering a range of phenomena into a risk – death, bankruptcy, litigation, an accident, a disease, a storm – through the specialized actuarial calculations available to them, and then offer guarantees against them. These phenomena would once have been accepted with fatalistic resignation: now they have become objects of risk, given value via the compensation that has been calculated for them (Ewald 1991). It is in this sense that anything can be a risk, if it is amenable to being turned into a risk through insurantial discourse, or any other kind of discourse directed at identifying and managing risk (ibid.: 200). Participation in insurance is about conducting one's life as an enterprise, to ensure that even when misfortune occurs, it has been planned for. It is, however, a socialized rather than wholly individualized approach, for insurance distributes the burden of risk among a large population and is underpinned by a notion of social rights in which members of an association agree to accept responsibility for each other's burdens (Dean 1999).

The second type of risk rationality is epidemiological risk, in which the calculus of risk is undertaken by bringing together assessment of a range of abstract factors with the incidence of health outcomes in targeted populations. Epidemiological risk adopts a similar approach to insurantial risk, but has a different target – illness and disease rather than loss of capital. Epidemiological techniques involve the tracing of illness and disease in specified populations using statistical and screening techniques, linking illness and disease with their causal variables in the attempt to predict health outcomes at the population level and thus to better control them and reduce health risks (Dean 1997: 218).

In the past, epidemiological risk strategies tended to be directed not at individuals' behaviours, but rather at altering environmental conditions in the attempt to improve health at the population level. Thus, for example, nineteenth-century public health endeavours sought to tackle hygiene and sanitary conditions in the city, such as air and water quality and sewerage arrangements, to reduce the incidence of epidemic diseases. While this focus on environmental health continues to some extent in the twenty-first century, there has developed a far greater emphasis on individuals' 'lifestyle' choices in relation to health status (Lupton 1995). Epidemiological risk factors are now often used to exhort individuals to engage in self-regulation. Thus, for example, if a certain population group is identified through statistical calculations as being at 'high risk' of developing heart disease, based on such attributes as gender, age and diet, then members of that group are then encouraged to deal with the risk factors themselves. This process does not necessarily involve consultations and examination of individuals by health professionals, but rather often takes place through mass-targeted media campaigns which rely on individuals identifying themselves as being 'at risk' and taking steps voluntarily to reduce their exposure to risk (ibid.). This is an example of 'government at a distance', for it relies upon voluntary participation in technologies of self-surveillance and a sense of self-responsibility rather than direct intervention.

The third type of risk rationality, case-management risk, is linked to clinical practice with individuals deemed to be threatening or disruptive in some way to the social order (the mad, the unemployed, the criminal, the dysfunctional, the poor, the long-term unemployed). Risk calculation in this type involves the qualitative assessment of risk for individuals and groups who are deemed to be 'at risk' (Dean 1997: 17). In contrast to the other two types of risk rationalities, the case-management approach uses more individualistic sources of data derived from interaction with and observation of specific clients, such as interviews, case-notes and files. Once risk is assessed, techniques for managing it on the part of the relevant experts (for example, social workers, health workers, and police officers) are brought into play. These include therapeutic practices directed at self-help through expert assistance, pedagogic practices designed to train dangerous others, and more coercive measures such as detainment and imprisonment, removing the 'risky' individuals from society (ibid.: 217–18).

Population-based risk strategies, however, also now enter the clinical arena. When patients visit their doctors, for example, their symptoms are not only treated as specific to them as individuals, but as manifestations of the patient's location in a wider socio-demographic context. In this way, epidemiological calculations about the likelihood of the occurrence of a condition in a given population are implemented upon the bodies of individuals, by applying risk categories derived from large-scale data sets. The case-management approach that is central to clinical strategies, with its emphasis on individual pathology and therapeutic intervention, is brought together with epidemiological risk, with its emphasis on indirect intervention via populations (Dean 1997).

Case-management types of risk rationality have proliferated in neo-liberal societies, moving from the spheres of social work and clinical medicine to address such problems as unemployment and 'welfare dependency'. The language of risk is taking over from that of need or welfare in the literature on personal social services, such as probation, mental health and child-care services, with risk assessment, risk management, the monitoring of risk and risk-taking itself having become the *raison d'être* and organizing principle of agencies providing such services. Risk-related discourses and strategies have taken on a key role in decision-making about service delivery, including the rationing of services and decisions about need (Dean 1997).

For all three types of risk rationalities, individuals and groups are increasingly expected to engage in practices identified as ways of avoiding or minimizing the impact of risks to themselves. This approach has been called by critics the 'new prudentialism', a neo-conservative approach which progressively removes the responsibility for risk protection from state agencies – as embodied in social insurance for such misfortunes as unemployment and ill health – and places it in the hands of the individual or community-based groups (O'Malley 1992; Dean 1997, 1999). As a result, the concept of risk has become more privatized and linked ever more closely to the concept of the entrepreneurial subject, calling into question the very notion of social rights: 'Here, we witness the "multiple responsibilization" of individuals, families, households and communities, for their own risks – of physical and mental ill health, of unemployment, of poverty in old age, of poor educational performance, of becoming victims of crime'. (Dean 1997: 218).

For example, in several neo-liberal societies there has been an increasing focus on the importance of individuals managing their own risks by taking out private insurance rather than participating in the social insurance schemes offered by the state. The latter served to offer security through the spreading of the costs of unfortunate events among the general population, so that risk was socialized. In doing so, it deflected attention away from those designated as being 'at risk', providing them with a security net rather than exhorting them to change their behaviour. In contrast, private insurance arrangements place the onus on individuals to take responsibility for insuring themselves against misfortune. It is accompanied by a range of other risk strategies that remove the responsibility for managing and dealing with risk from the state (Dean 1997).

Under the 'new prudentialism' dispositif, the acceptance of personal responsibility is presented as a practice of freedom, relief from state intervention, an opportunity for the entrepreneurial subject to make choices about the conduct of her or his life. More and more domains of life are identified as amenable to and requiring of these choices. In the context of neo-liberal democracies, which value self-autonomy over direct state intervention, these strategies are seen both to work to minimize risks and to protect individuals' rights. In this context, the role of government is to provide advice and assistance for the self-management of risks, encouraging the active, free citizen who voluntarily engages in risk avoidance, rather than providing large-scale financial support.

Contemporary technologies of risk calculation and control, therefore, comprise one aspect of a change in ways of viewing the role of society. What 'the social' is understood to be has changed from notions of a mass collectivity to dynamic smaller groupings. We are progressively understanding and acting upon ourselves not as members of a specific society or through the ethos of the welfare state, but as self-actualizing individuals who move between loose and fluid social aggregations, taking up different roles in each. Small community or affiliation-based groupings are set in place to deal with such phenomena as risk, which have limited and dynamic constituencies and interests (Dean 1997, 1999, 2007). This is taking place in a sociocultural and historical context in which dominant notions of selfhood privilege the self who is able to exert strong control over her or his mind and body, constantly engages in self-examination, is able to engage in self-denial for the greater good and readily takes up the injunctions of experts in making lifestyle choices. Those individuals who are deemed to be at 'high risk' either of being a victim of risk or of perpetrating risk are expected to take control to prevent risk through their own actions rather than rely on social insurance apparatuses as a safety-net.

This representation of the individual is that of *homo economicus,* a subject who is invested with additional moral and political characteristics and conforms to the self-interested and responsible actor found in neo-conservative discourses. Situational crime discourse, for example, represents the potential offender as a universal 'abiographical individual', a 'rational choice' actor who weighs up the pros and cons before committing an offence. So too, victims are understood as rational choice actors, with the responsibility to protect themselves. It is therefore regarded as their fault if they become vulnerable to crime (O'Malley 1992: 264–6).

As the welfare state is wound back, there is less incentive for the state to provide social insurance schemes such as unemployment benefits or socialized health insurance: 'in the present era, the success of programs inspired by economic rationalists and neo-conservatism has been stripping away socialized risk management, and replacing it with a programmatic combination of privatized prudentialism and punitive sovereignty' (O'Malley 1992: 261). The lack of interest in the biography or motivation of the 'at risk' individual deflects attention away from the socio-economic underpinnings of risk, and divorces misfortune from questions of social justice. This leads back to the early modern risk strategies of coercion and punishment and the construction of new 'dangerous classes' requiring active surveillance and disciplining. It appears that societies dominated by neo-liberal politics in the late modern era are returning to previous forms of discipline in relation to individuals and social groups that are identified as being 'at risk' or imposing a risk upon others. In relation to crime prevention, for example, the broader social structural underpinnings of crime, such as socio-economic disadvantage, is ignored in favour of strategies that are punitive for those who are seen to lack self-control (ibid.: 265).

PRECAUTIONARY RISK AND THE CRISIS OF NEO-LIBERALISM

Since the advent of the twenty-first century, and in the wake of a series of catastrophic events that occurred in the first decade of this century, governmentality scholars have turned their attention to how neo-liberalist forms of government have dealt with these disasters. In his recent work, Dean (2010) has commented on the challenges to neo-liberalism posed by such events as the 11 September 2001 terrorist attacks and other terrorist attacks and bombings in Madrid, Bali and London, the emergence of trans-species infectious diseases such as the swine and avian influenza pandemics, Hurricane Katrina, the Asian tsunami, climate change and the global financial crisis, which in turn have resulted in financial insecurity and political unrest in many developed countries. These events were unanticipated and catastrophic. Dean asserts that many of these events were viewed as exceptional and extraordinary but in hindsight could be analysed as anticipated.

In their extraordinary effects and potential to radically disrupt everyday life, catastrophes are different from and more serious than the emergencies and disasters that have preoccupied risk society and in response to which governmental measures have previously been developed (Anderson 2010; Aradau and van Munster 2012). The future has now become even more open than before because of the complexity of the ceaseless associations and configurations of diverse and heterogeneous elements in assemblages of transnational flows and connections. These assemblages are now dynamic and non-linear and it has become necessary to act on the beginnings of catastrophes before they can eventuate. Governments and the mass media have become preoccupied with developing anticipatory actions to deal with the next catastrophe (Anderson 2010), forcing policy-makers to grapple with the apparent impossible dilemmas of how to 'think the unthinkable', 'know the unknowable' or 'expect the unexpected' (Aradau and van Munster 2012: 99).

The concept of 'precautionary risk' has developed in response to the combination of scientific uncertainty and the anticipation of the possibility of serious and irreversible damage (Aradau and van Munster 2007, 2012; Anderson 2010; Dean 2010; Oels 2011). Precautionary risk is a new risk dispositif which has been added to or modified older technologies of risk management and thereby reconfigured them. It inscribes other forms of calculation to the future in a context in which catastrophic risks that are incalculable must be governed. This risk dispositif thus demands that precautions are undertaken even in the face of great uncertainty. It is derived from environmental politics – the first area where risks were catastrophic but incalculable and potentially unmanageable (Aradau and van Munster 2007, 2012). From the precautionary risk perspective, risks are viewed as contingent, constantly shifting in their form. It is therefore impossible to determine 'safe' levels (Oels 2011). In relation to such threats as terrorism, what Aradau and van Munster (2007: 91) refer to as 'an insatiable quest for knowledge' has eventuated, involving such practices as profiling populations, continual surveillance, the gathering of biometric data and intelligence and developing strategies for the management and prevention of catastrophes. These strategies actively attempt to identify and manage situations that may become catastrophic in the future.

There are four interlinked governmental rationalities involved in precautionary risk: zero risk, worst case scenario, shifting the burden of proof, and serious irreversible damage (Munster 2007: 103). Under the concept of precautionary risk, any level of risk other than zero-level risk is considered unacceptable and thus a justifiable target of intervention. Precautionary risk calculations and strategies attempt to govern the ungovernable. Although uncertainty exists about the calculability of risks, it is considered that precautions must still be taken to avert the potentially catastrophic results. For precautionary risk rationalities, what has happened in the past may be no longer relevant to the unpredictable and constantly shifting nature of an open future (Anderson 2010).

Anderson (2010: 786–7) has identified three modes of anticipatory practice which allow futures to be rendered present while remaining absent: calculation, imagination and performance. Thus, for example, in relation to the threat of a newly emergent infectious disease, multiple catastrophe models have been developed to predict the outcome of thousands of possible pandemics based on such features as lethality and infectiousness of a virus, the spatial and temporal location of an outbreak, the efficacy of counter-measures and the life-cycle of an infection (ibid.: 784). Imaginative strategies such as visioning, future-planning and scenario planning are also employed as part of the dispositif of precautionary risk to identify 'worst case' scenarios and develop methods for reducing vulnerability to such events. Future events are imagined as if they were real, using forms of visualization and narratives that depict what a future world would look like in the event of a specific catastrophe. In addition, strategies of performance such as acting, role-play, gaming or simulations may be used in the attempt to imagine which catastrophes might be experienced and dealt with. These risk strategies differ from older calculative rationalities in their reliance on creative imagining of hypothetical scenarios (Aradau and van Munster 2007; Anderson 2010).

The lack of prescience on the part of the developed world in anticipating the disastrous events occurring in the early twenty-first century as 'risky phenomena' and mobilizing to prevent them has resulted in an ontological challenge to the neo-liberal metanarratives of economic progress, peace and freedom. This has instigated a 'crisis of neo-liberalism' (Dean 2010: 462), whereby governmental agencies and institutions have been forced to recognize their failure to control risk. The model of rationally predicting the future has reached its limit in response to unknowable catastrophic threats. Many of the tenets held dear to neo-liberalist philosophy and modes of governance, such as self-entrepreneurialism, the free market and free trade, have been called into question by the catastrophic events referred to above. The unforeseen catastrophe has introduced a radical uncertainty about the future and about how best to govern. States must consequently deal with the question of the extent of governance, avoiding both governing too much and governing too little in the attempt to deal with unexpected risk events (Anderson 2010; Dean 2010). This may involve excessive state intervention and a suspension or curtailment of traditional neoliberal modes of governance, including the winding back of fundamental liberties and basic citizen rights. These measures were initially brought into being as part of a 'state of emergency' but appear to have become entrenched as part of what ex-American vice-president Dick Cheney described as the 'new normalcy' (Dean 2010: 464).

Unlike insurantial risk, in which it was the behaviour of the insured that was viewed as causing risk and governed in the attempt to preserve the zero-risk imperative, precautionary risk holds the dangerous Other as responsible for risk. Far from the cosmopolitan and democratic acceptance of the Other posited by Beck as emerging in world risk society (Chapter 4), precautionary risk technologies position everyone as potentially a threat, but especially those from 'suspicious' ethnic groups or those with a certain appearance suggesting that they have a Middle Eastern heritage, for example. The precautionary risk dispositif is used to reintroduce such overtly coercive measures as pre-emptive strikes, torture and indefinite detention of suspected terrorists, as well as more discrete surveillance technologies of all citizens in such sites as airports to deal with the uncertainties of the risk of terrorism (Aradau and van Munster, 2007). So too, the global financial crisis has resulted in the emergence of a renewed sovereign power on the part of governments, who have directly intervened in free market and banking system using such measures as financial bailouts and infrastructure spending (Dean 2010).

CONCLUDING COMMENTS

This chapter has highlighted the ways in which the concept of risk, employed to address governmental concerns, has contributed to the production of certain kinds of rationalities, strategies and subjectivities. It has been argued that according to the Foucauldian perspective, risk strategies, technologies, knowledges and discourses – risk dispositifs – are the means of ordering the social and material worlds through methods of rationalization and calculation, attempts to render disorder and uncertainty more controllable. It is these strategies and discourses that bring risk into being, that select certain phenomena as being 'risky' and therefore requiring management, either by institutions or individuals.

The accounts provided by Foucauldian scholars of risk have shown that it is not simply a matter of risk becoming less calculable, or shifting from local to global contexts, as the 'risk society' thesis would have it (Dean 1999). Rather, changes in risk rationalities have occurred which have resulted in risk being conceptualized and dealt with in diverse ways that have strong links to ideas about how individuals should deport themselves in relation to the state. Some of those taking up a Foucauldian perspective have remarked upon changes in the governance of risk occurring towards the end of the last century, in which there is far less reliance upon social insurance and far more upon individual self-management and self-protection from risk. This is an outcome of the political ethos of neo-liberalism, which emphasizes minimal intervention on the part of the state and emphasizes 'self-help' and individual autonomy for citizens. These risk rationalities have themselves begun to make way for others in the context of a catastrophic start to the new century, where twentieth-century philosophies and strategies of neo-liberalism have been challenged, tested and in some cases relinquished for a return to more sovereign modes of government.

Foucault himself and those taking up his perspectives on the regulation of subjects via the discourses of governmentality may be criticized for devoting too much attention to these discourses and strategies and not enough to how people actually respond to them as part of their everyday lives. The question of how risk-related discourses and strategies operate, how they may be taken up, negotiated or resisted by those who are the subject of them, remains under-examined. Some critics have asserted that governmentality studies demonstrate a reluctance to acknowledge the 'real' and move beyond a focus on policy-oriented or media textual data sources and direct attention at contestation and politics. They argue that governmentality risk studies should acknowledge context more specifically, including greater recognition of the ways in which government operates from below as well as from above (Lippert and Stenson 2010). The governmentality approach has also been criticized for its strong constructionist perspective and for not acknowledging that harmful phenomena exist (whether or not they are called 'risks') and that they have real consequences for people. It has further been taken to task for not allowing for the possibility of political action and resistance (Rigakos and Law 2009).

As is the case of the subject constructed in the 'risk society' thesis put forward by Beck and Giddens, the Foucauldian view of the self has been critiqued for its tendency to represent this subject as universal, without recognizing differences between the ways in which people of different gender, age, ethnicity, and so on may be treated by and respond to these discourses and strategies. Some scholars have questioned how people transform themselves into reflexive subjects by applying rational programmes or imperatives to embodied habitual and affective sensibilities and habits. They assert that people do not always behave like the rational, calculating subjects of governmentality theory, and that it is important to understand how the pre-reflexive and the reflexive operate together when interpreting how individuals respond to risk discourses (Wilkinson 2006; Binkley 2009). The next chapter takes up these questions, looking at how people respond to risk in the contexts of their everyday lives and located within particular social structures, power relations and sub-groups.

6

RISK AND SUBJECTIVITY

The theoretical perspectives on risk that have been reviewed thus far provide various approaches to understanding how concepts of risk influence subjectivity. For the 'cultural/symbolic' approach, risk is used to reproduce and maintain concepts of selfhood and group membership, particularly in defining self from the polluting or 'risky' Other. For the 'risk society' perspective, reflexive awareness and concern about risk pervade modern sensibilities, creating new forms of relating to the self and others, including experts and institutions. For the 'governmentality' perspective, risk dispositifs contribute to the configuring of a particular type of subject: the autonomous, self-regulating moral agent who voluntarily takes up governmental imperatives. While these insights are important in the abstract theorizing of risk responses, the writers following these perspectives have tended not to explore in detail the diverse and dynamic ways in which lay people respond to risk.

This chapter looks at how lay people engage reflexively or otherwise with risk. In doing so, the discussion frequently draws on the empirical findings of studies exploring the ways in which people construct their risk knowledges in the context of their everyday lives. The chapter begins with a review of risk knowledges and reflexivity. It then goes on to explore the importance of social structures and power relations and finally the role of aesthetic, affective or hermeneutic judgements and habituation in people's responses to risk.

RISK KNOWLEDGES AND REFLEXIVITY

Late at night on 30 July 1997, 18 people were killed when a landslide occurred at Thredbo village, a popular ski resort in the alpine area of Australia. A ski lodge collapsed and slipped down a steep slope, falling onto a second lodge and crushing the occupants of both. Only one occupant survived the incident, eventually being dug out by rescue workers after being entombed for days under a pile of concrete and rubble. This incident received a high level of national news media coverage, particularly in relation to the gradual recovery of the bodies of the dead from the wreckage of the lodges and the rescue of the sole survivor.

Six months later, the findings of a geotechnical study into the stability of other buildings in the area were released, identifying a number of other lodges as being 'at risk' of being damaged or destroyed in a similar landslip. A Sydney newspaper reported the reaction of one inhabitant of a lodge that was labelled as being 'at high risk'. She described her shock at this finding, saying that the lodge was 'our home' and that her husband and two daughters had never felt unsafe living there: 'We love living here. It's just beautiful. It's been very special to our kids. I have never felt unsafe here, so having words like "risk" being thrown around now is just devastating because we don't feel that risk. Even when the [July] slide happened, I never felt unsafe.' Another woman interviewed, who was staying at a lodge designated by the engineers who wrote the report as being 'at very high risk', said that she was not concerned by the finding: 'You go when your time is up,' she said. 'You could get killed on the road' (quoted in the *Sydney Morning Herald*, 31 December 1997).

As the psychometric literature has documented (Chapter 1), 'lay' people often hold perspectives on risk that differ from those put forward by 'experts'. But as Douglas has further contended (Chapter 3), this is not simply a matter of their 'ignorance' or inability to understand probabilities. The existence of varying perspectives on 'risk', among both experts and lay people, suggests that the phenomenon of risk is a production of competing knowledges about the world. The words of the first woman quoted above suggest, for example, that people may feel particularly safe in places in which they have chosen to live and bring up their families, with which they have an everyday familiarity, in sharp contrast to the assessments of experts. Alternatively, they may adopt a fatalistic approach, as articulated by the second woman quoted in the newspaper article. Both approaches have their own logic and rationale, and make eminent sense to those who adopt them as part of their views on life.

It was argued in earlier chapters that risk discourses configure social actors in certain specific ways. These discourses tend either to identify subjects as responsive to risks that are identified as threatening them, actively making choices in relation to risk prevention, or as risk-makers, the causes of risk, and thus requiring observation, regulation and discipline. As Beck and Giddens have pointed out (Chapter 4), as a consequence of modernization and individualization, increasingly more aspects of life are considered to be subject to human agency. The contemporary self, therefore, is placed in a position of making choices about a myriad of aspects of life, such that '[c]hoosing is the inescapable fate of our time' (Melucci 1996: 44). With an apparent openness of lifestyle come additional burdens, including the assumption of all the risks that go with decision-making. The complexity of living in a late modern world, in which change is rapid and intense and the number of choices to be made have proliferated, renders choice-making very difficult and fraught with uncertainty. People are expected to take personal responsibility for these choices, to follow their own interests. Hence the proliferation of risk discourses, which represent humans as far more able to exert control over their environment than they were in previous eras.

It is clear that many aspects of people's lives are influenced by their awareness of risk and the responsibilities involved with avoiding risks. It is also evident that individualization, which emphasizes personal responsibility for life outcomes, is dominant in late modern societies. Many people appear to have accepted the notion that one should make oneself aware of risks and act in accordance with experts' risk advice so as to prevent or reduce the impact of risk. Indeed, the notion that one is personally responsible for the control of risk appears to be acculturated very early in life. Research conducted by Green (1997) found that even among children as young as 7 years old, the notion that accidents can be prevented and must have a cause which can be used to blame someone, was very dominant. The English children in her study, ranging in age from 7 to 11, argued that accidents were more likely to be the result of known or knowable sets of risk factors than blameless and unpredictable events, and therefore in theory could be prevented through responsible and rational behaviour. Almost all the children accepted the responsibility for keeping themselves safe from harm and saw themselves as culpable if an accident happened to them. Their stories about engaging in risks or avoiding risks also served as signifiers for social identities and relationships beyond the meaning of accidental injury: representing oneself as a 'careful' or 'daring' person to one's friends, for example, as part of conforming to friendship group norms.

Accepting personal responsibility for risks and taking up experts' risk advice are not the only responses to risk, despite the claims of writers such as Beck and Giddens. The notion of reflexivity itself suggests a rational, calculating actor: people are portrayed as choosing rationally between various perspectives on risk provided by expert knowledge systems. It also appears to give credence to the role played by experts in constructing risk meanings over that of lay actors. The reflexivity thesis implies that individuals develop and exercise reflexivity in response to expert knowledge, rather than generating their own risk knowledges through their own experiences of the world. While they acknowledge that reflexivity is practised in the sphere of the intimate and the everyday, Giddens and Beck tend to suggest that this reflexivity is again primarily in response to expert knowledge systems. They give little recognition to the ways in which lay actors drawn upon their own situated knowledges of the world in constructing risk understandings and responding to experts' pronouncements on risk (Wynne 1996; Lupton and Tulloch 2002a, 2002b; Tulloch and Lupton 2003).

It has been argued by other commentators that while risks may be debated at the level of expertise and public accountability, they are dealt with by most individuals at the level of the local, the private, the everyday and the intimate. Lay knowledges tend to be far more contextual, localized and individualized, reflexively aware of diversity and change, than the universalizing tendencies of expert knowledges (Wynne 1996: 70). Lash and Wynne (1992; see also Wynne 1996) highlight what they see as the multi-layered response to risk on the part of lay people as a form of 'private reflexivity' which, they argue, must be the basis for the more public forms of reflexivity (that is, debate about risk at the political level).

Some sociologists have sought to demonstrate that lay perceptions of risk are founded on sources of knowledge that should be acknowledged as being equally as important and rational as scientific expert assessments, which themselves are often based on 'optimistic fantasies about behaviour in the real world' (Wynne 1989: 39). Their argument tends to revolve around debates concerning the supposed 'irrationality' of lay people's responses to risk, contending that what may seem 'irrational' is in fact based on rational judgement. Members of the lay public also incorporate into their assessment of risk their pre-established knowledge of how the relevant industries and regulatory bodies have tended to deal with risks in the past (Wynne 1989, 1996). People make judgements about the persuasiveness and trustworthiness of experts, involving recognition of the sociocultural frames and interests which shape experts' risk knowledges. Rather than this knowledge being a 'distorting' factor in lay assessment, it is an important element in their judgement of risk.

Jensen and Blok (2008) attempted to test Beck's theories concerning environmental risk in their study of the health and environmental concerns stemming from the use of pesticides in farming in Denmark, using interviews and focus groups. They note that while many people spoke about the risks of pesticides, the respondents demonstrated multi-layered and often ambivalent attitudes to the notion of pesticides as 'risky'. They acknowledged the needs of farmers to use them as part of modern farming methods. Thus, while the respondents expressed views that might be predicted by Beck's risk society thesis, they also articulated counter-views, sometimes based on social solidarity with such groups as farmers, particularly those struggling economically. They acknowledged their dependence on expert opinion, and that this kind of risk expertise is necessary and irreplaceable, but also their awareness that technico-scientific knowledges may be contradictory or wrong. Trust in experts was conditional upon whether they were regarded as authoritative, based on which institution they were affiliated with, for example. The respondents also drew upon their own embodied knowledge of pesticides in forming their judgments, referring to their own experiences using their senses. Thus, for example, they made reference to the 'bad' or 'synthetic' smell of pesticides or the appearance of the countryside when pesticides had been used.

As such research suggests, it is therefore not simply a matter of individuals weighing up the relative magnitude of physical risks as different experts assess them. Rather, they go through a process of evaluating risk experts and institutions themselves. Such responses are not merely individualistic rationalist-calculative assessments of science, but are shaped through sociocultural processes. Individuals' responses reflect different ways of understanding and representing such phenomena as agency, predictability, control and values. As members of social groups and networks, people's responses to risk are embedded within these relationships, and are therefore collective as well as developed through individual biographies (Wynne 1989, 1996).

People also develop a 'collective memory' about risks, based largely on mass media coverage but also on informal discussions with each other. For example, it is evident that 'collective memory' underpinned Spanish newspaper accounts of the avian flu pandemic that affected the world in the early years of this century. In the newspaper accounts the devastating Spanish flu pandemic that appeared in the years immediately following World War I was recounted as a narrative matrix, or a narrative pattern, used to make sense of avian influenza and to dramatize its risks. As this earlier pandemic was known to have caused tens of millions of deaths worldwide, drawing an analogy with it represented the avian flu epidemic as potentially catastrophic and uncontrollable (Mairal 2011). Previous fatal influenza outbreaks including the Spanish and Hong Kong flu pandemics were also frequently referenced in British news media reports of avian flu (Nerlich and Halliday 2007). So too, responses to the global financial crisis beginning in 2008 and the subsequent Eurozone economic crisis have drawn comparisons with the Great Depression of the 1930s. The effects of this Depression resonated worldwide in ways that are still current in many older people's memories and in the consciousness of their children, who heard their parents recount stories of the hardships many people suffered during this time (Miller 2010).

Lay actors also often resist or directly challenge experts' judgements on risk. In constructing private reflexivity, people struggle with the reconciliation of different and often conflicting interests and identities: they 'informally but incessantly problematise their own relationships with expertise of all kinds, as part of their negotiation of their own identities' (Wynne 1996: 50). Even where there seems to be no evidence of public dissent over risk, at the everyday, personal level, such dissent constantly takes place. This suggests that the relationship that people have with 'expert' knowledge systems is highly complex and ambivalent. It is not simply a question of lay people deciding which of two or more bodies of dissenting expert knowledge to trust when they are making judgements about risk. Rather, they construct their own expert knowledges, with or without the use of risk professionals' knowledge (ibid.).

Lay people are aware of their dependency on expert knowledge when it comes to disputes about risk. They are also aware of their lack of agency and opportunity, as 'non-experts', to challenge expert knowledges, even if the expert knowledge is uncertain or conflicting (Wynne 1996; Michael 1996). In the context of their everyday lives, aspects of expert knowledge may be considered irrelevant or distracting. What is considered to be 'ignorance' on the part of experts may be thought of by lay actors as a deliberate ignoring or avoidance of expert knowledge because it is regarded as essentially peripheral to the key issues at stake, or at worst, inaccurate and misleading. 'Ignorance' on the part of lay people becomes a positive and agential choice in these cases, not a passive deficit requiring greater access to expert knowledges (Michael 1996: 119–20).

Sociological research investigating the ways in which logics of risk are established, maintained or revised as part of individuals' location within specific sociocultural settings points to the complexities and ambiguities of such knowledge formation. It shows that these alternative rationalities, typically portrayed by experts as inaccurate or irrational, often make sense in the context of an individual's life situation, including the cultural frameworks and meanings that shape subjectivity and social relations and the institutions and social structures within which individuals are placed. The reflexivity of lay people in relation to risk may develop from their observations of the ways in which everyday life operates and from conversations and interactions with other lay actors. For example, people may develop a fatalistic attitude towards risk because they have observed that life does not always 'play by the rules'. Someone who drinks heavily and smokes may live to a ripe old age, while an ascetic non-smoking, jogging vegetarian may die young. Most people can cite such examples among the people they know (Davison *et al.* 1992). Conforming to expert advice about how to avoid risk, therefore, is seen not necessarily to guarantee protection from harm. If fate steps in, preventive action is seen to be useless.

Risk positions not only emerge from people's locations within social milieux, but also serve to position them within such milieux, as a means of developing and supporting social cohesion or group membership (Macgill 1989: 57). Risk positions, therefore, may also be important to people's sense of self-identity as part of a social group or sub-culture. People who live in areas designated as 'high risk', for example, may define themselves positively as 'survivors' or 'battlers', as part of a community that has chosen to ignore experts' warnings and continue to live in these areas (as exemplified by the women from Thredbo referred to at the beginning of this chapter). Concerns about risks often generate temporary political alliances between people, united by their anxieties and their desire to fight against the agencies they see as imposing the risk upon them. So too, those who voluntarily engage in risk-taking, such as mountain climbers and parachuters (or even, these days, cigarette smokers), may see the shared challenge as a unifying force (see Chapter 8). It is important to note, however, that rather than remaining static, risk rationalities are often constantly shifting and changing in response to changes in personal experience, local knowledge networks and expert knowledges.

Qualitative research carried out on the everyday aspects of risk perceptions and risk understandings in a variety of Western countries has demonstrated that people's concepts of risk often interlace pre-modern notions of fate and lack of control with late modern notions of reflexive control over risk. Further, people tend not to have an overarching, all-pervasive fear of risk. The risks they identify are highly discrete and contextual to their personal biographies (Smith *et al.* 2006; Lupton and Tulloch 2002b; Tulloch and Lupton 2003). For example, in a Swedish study, researchers conducted focus groups about risk with people in rural and urban areas and with people from a foreign background and experts in risk management. They found that the participants tended not to be concerned about 'new' risks such as those experts have identified as related to climate change and global warming. Rather, the participants were worried about phenomena they identified as risks from personal experiences and life contexts such as their workplace and family. They thus had a more traditional rather than a reflexive approach to risk, particularly the immigrant and rural groups (Olofsson and Ohman 2007).

Other commentators have argued that the incalculability and uncertainty of risk in contemporary society, where insurantial approaches can no longer apply to many risks because they cannot be statistically calculated, have led in some areas of the world ridden by political conflict to a concept of risk that pre-dates risk society. It has been claimed that people in troubled zones such as the Occupied Territories of the West Bank and Gaza Strip are reverting to a fatalistic approach to risk, feeling as if they have lost control over risk and are no longer able to protect themselves against it. The neo-liberal ideal of the entrepreneurial citizen who manages her or his own exposure to risk and choice of risk management providers becomes meaningless in this social context. A fundamentalist perspective gains credence as religious belief appears to offer a source of hope and guarantee of protection from dangers. Thus, in the Occupied Territories, the fundamentalist Hamas group has gained followers. For such citizens, the rationality of risk no longer exists: their conduct is not managed by prudential calculations or self-management of risk but by coercion, oppression and exclusion (Gordon and Filc 2005).

These observations support Giddens' observations on the emergence of fundamentalism discussed in Chapter 4.

It may be speculated that people in Western countries that have experienced significant economic downturns in the wake of the global financial crisis, such as Greece, Spain and Ireland, in what has been termed the 'Eurozone crisis', may also find themselves turning towards a more fatalistic approach to risk, in a context in which previous privileged notions of the risk-avoiding individual who is able to prosper have lost their meaning.

SOCIAL STRUCTURES AND POWER RELATIONS

The approach to risk behaviours which assumes rational calculation, the weighing up of costs and benefits, also tends to ignore the role played by power relations. Individuals are represented as agential, operating in fields of social relations in which they are able to move between different logics of risk at will. Some critics have responded to Beck's and Giddens' writings on risk by asking whether reflexivity is an important aspect of everyday subjectivity for most people in late modern societies. They have drawn attention, in particular, to what they consider to be the continuing influence of social class, gender, ethnicity, position in the life course, and so on in shaping subjectivity and individuals' life chances. While these broader structuring factors may have weakened somewhat in their influence in the contemporary era, particularly in the move towards individualization, it is argued that they are still important.

The designation of the label 'at risk' often serves to reinforce the marginalized or powerless status of individuals. Certain social groups have tended to be singled out as 'at risk' of a constellation of harms – children and young people, members of the working class, pregnant women, people who use illicit drugs, the elderly, sex workers, the homeless, the mentally ill. The 'at risk' label tends either to position members of these social groups as particularly vulnerable, passive, powerless or weak, or as particularly dangerous to themselves or others. In both cases, special attention is directed at these social groups, positioning them in a network of surveillance, monitoring and intervention.

The self-reflexive individual, as presented by Beck and Giddens, is a socially and economically privileged person who has the cultural and material resources to engage in self-inspection. Many people, however, simply lack the resources and techniques with which to engage in the project of self-reflexivity. Lash (1994; Lash and Urry 1994) sees Beck's reflexive modernization thesis as having at its core the assumption that agency is progressively freeing from structure, that people are increasingly able to define their own lives. He questions this, however, claiming that rather than structuring factors disappearing entirely, new ones are generated in late modernity. The important social structures of early modernity – such as the family, the welfare state, trade unions, government bureaucracy, and social class – have been largely replaced by information and communication structures.

Lash argues, therefore, like the governmentality writers, that: 'The risk society is thus not so much about the distribution of "bads" or dangers as about a mode of conduct centred on risk' (1994: 141). As such, there might be said to be a distinction between 'reflexivity winners' and 'reflexivity losers'. The former are those who are equipped through access to social resources such as education to engage in self-reflexivity, while the latter are those people who are unemployed or otherwise socially underprivileged. As Lash asks:

> Just how 'reflexive' is it possible for a single mother in an urban ghetto to be?... Just how much freedom from the 'necessity' of 'structure' and structural poverty does this ghetto mother have to self-construct her own 'life narratives'?
>
> (Lash 1994: 120)

He argues that access to and place in the new modes of information and communication structures are now more important to people's life chances than is their access to productive capital. Those who are not equipped to acquire new forms of information and access to knowledge flows, or who are excluded from acquisition, are those who are 'reflexivity losers'.

Feminist critics have contended that the writings of Giddens and Beck, particularly in relation to marriage, the family, intimacy and the labour market in the context of late modernity, fail to fully acknowledge the constraints that gender expectations still play in shaping the life course. This work tends to assume a disembodied male subject in their focus on rational life planning and negotiation of decision-making. Beck and Giddens make broad, sweeping statements about 'society', 'the reflexive self', 'the family' and 'gender relations' with little recognition of the interplay between the state, gender, the private sphere and social class. They have little to say about relationships which are not heterosexual, position the private sphere as the natural location of women, fail to recognize reproductive labour and represent gender as a fixed characteristic rather than a social relation and performative. Nor do they recognize the continuing constraints faced by women because of their gender in achieving self-actualization (Lewis and Bennett 2003; Green and Singleton 2006; Brooks 2008; Mulinari and Sandell 2009).

Thus, for example, in her interviews with successful professional women working in academia and corporations and living in Hong Kong and Singapore, Brooks (2008) found little evidence that gender was becoming less of a structuring force in the women's lives. These women were highly aware of the competing demands of work and family life and how these constrained their choices. Brooks argues that the claims of Beck and Giddens about the 'freeing' of individuals from the constraints of gender role, the gender-neutral career identity and the opportunity for people to make their own biographies outside of these roles and expectations therefore were overstated. So too, Green and Singleton's (2006) interviews with young British women of white and South Asian ethnicity found that both gender and ethnicity were significant structuring forces shaping these women's leisure activities. They comment that emotions, actions and calculations related to risk are temporally and spatially located and deeply embedded within normative assumptions about female 'respectability'. Thus, for example, both the young South Asian and the white women found it difficult to go out into public spaces at night because of concerns about their safety. The night-time public spaces to which they had access in their town were represented as hazardous to young women because of the threat of physical assault from men. The South Asian young women in particular avoided going out of the home after dark, both because of fears of their physical safety and strict cultural expectations about the need for them to stay at home and participate in women-only activities.

John Tulloch and I (Lupton and Tulloch 2002a, 2002b; Tulloch and Lupton 2003) found in our own interviews with Britons and Australians that they demonstrated a heightened awareness of risk and viewed it as emerging across a wide range of domains, including financial, health, criminal, intimate and work-related. As such, our interviewees did conform to the archetype of the risk-aware, reflexive subject who chooses to seek out information on risks and weigh up their options in terms of how to avoid the phenomena they had identified as 'risks'. Our interviewees also expressed opinions that conformed to Beck's theory of individualization, in commenting on the loss of tradition in structuring life choices and pathways and the sense that 'community' was being undermined. However, the interviewees from both Britain and Australia also demonstrated a politicized consciousness of the structural causes of risk. They emphasized the importance of government intervention in protecting people from risk and the role played by social disadvantage in exposing people to risk. Their responses were mediated by such factors as age, gender, occupation, ethnicity or nationality and sexual identity.

Some of the most interesting work on the power relations and social contexts in which risk is understood and acted upon has been undertaken in relation to the activities of marginalized groups such as sex workers and gay men. One example is female and male prostitutes working on the streets, who often lack the power to enforce safer sex practices upon their clients, even though they are highly aware of the risk of contracting HIV/AIDS and feel susceptible to infection. They are also vulnerable to violent attacks on them by their clients and others (Leaker and Dunk-West 2011). Sex workers like 'rent boys', who lack permanent accommodation and are ill-paid for their work, may often choose temporary comforts such as a warm place to sleep and a hot meal that unprotected sex with a punter may afford them over the more distant risk of contracting HIV (Hart and Boulton 1995). Access to material resources, therefore, may be a central feature of risk behaviours. A study of female sex workers who worked from flats (rather than on the streets) demonstrated the importance of social context and the organization and conditions of work for these individuals' risk practices. The women's social status, their position as a marginalized group given little protection by the police or other authorities, meant that they were forced to develop strategies among themselves to deal with the risks of physical violence, robbery and abuse from their clients. This included working with other women who act as gatekeepers, helping to maintain control over the interaction by monitoring the clients and the time they spent with the women (Whittaker and Hart 1996). Female sex workers at risk of assault from clients often tend to position themselves as responsible for protecting themselves, despite lack of control over the conditions in which they work (Leaker and Dunk-West 2011).

Such studies reveal that people's social location and their access to material resources are integral to the ways in which they conceptualize and deal with risk. Rather than responding as autonomous agents to the risks they perceive, people act as members of social groups and social networks. Their membership of these groups and networks may well be more dynamic than was the case in earlier eras, but it is still influential in mediating the capacities of individuals to act as reflexive subjects in relation to risk.

AESTHETIC, AFFECTIVE AND HABITUAL DIMENSIONS

In a further critique of Becks and Giddens' model of reflexivity in late modernity, it has been argued that their approach leaves aside the cultural and aesthetic aspects of judgement: 'Their idea of the subject is an entity that reflexively controls bodies rather than as something which itself is bodily' (Lash and Urry 1994: 32). It has been contended that reflexivity should be understood not simply as a process of rationalist self-monitoring through cognitive or normative categories. Reflexivity may also incorporate self-interpretation and interpretation of social processes, conducted through aesthetic and hermeneutic understandings, those that seek to understand the deep meaning and significance of actions, words, deeds and institutions (Lash 1993, 2000).

Aesthetic or hermeneutic reflexivity is embodied in such aspects of life as taste and style, sense of time and space, consumption, leisure and popular culture and membership of sub-cultural groups. It is rooted in background assumptions and unarticulated practices and in intuition, feeling, emotion and the spiritual. This type of reflexivity involves the processing of signs and symbols rather than simply 'information'. It is a product of an individual's embodied 'being-in-the-world', in which knowledge about the world is developed through – and not just in relation to – the body

(Merleau-Ponty 1962). Aesthetic reflexivity relies upon an individual's membership of a community, the moral and culturally learnt and shared assumptions, preferences and categories to which Douglas refers in her work on risk (See Chapter 3). Aesthetic and hermeneutic reflexivity is not rooted in self-monitoring, but rather in self-interpretation, involving intuition and the imagination above moral and cognitive judgement. It pre-exists the development of moral and cognitive judgements, and is based in bodily predispositions that are acculturated from individuals' entry into society (Lash 1993, 2000; Binkley 2009).

An example of the hermeneutic dimension of risk responses is the ways in which many people define others as 'risky', as posing a threat to them in some way. Many studies have shown that people tend to deal with the risk of HIV/AIDS and other sexually transmissible diseases by constructing categories of riskiness based not necessarily or only on expert definitions but on their culturally acquired understandings of purity and danger. People who are thought to be 'clean' – based on judgements of such attributes as their social class, ethnicity, sexual preference, how long one has known them, their manner and physical appearance – are treated as less risky, while those who are symbolically 'dirty' – again based on consideration of the attributes listed above – are designated and treated as posing a threat to oneself, as contaminating. A study of young Canadians, for example, found that they tended to categorize potential sexual partners as 'risky' or otherwise based on consideration of how well known they were to the interviewee, where and how they first met them, whether they were judged to be 'sleazy' or not and their appearance. The primary mode of selection was choosing someone who was not the 'wrong kind of person'. If an individual was defined as 'not risky', based on these considerations, they were considered not to be likely to carry sexually transmissible disease and were therefore trusted as safe to have sex with (Maticka-Tyndale 1992). The assumptions on which these judgements of 'riskiness' are based are founded in binary oppositions, stereotypes and other systems of meaning that individuals begin to learn from childhood as part of their acculturation into society (see Chapter 7 for further discussion of risk and Otherness.)

While lay people may be positioned by experts as lacking rational judgement on risks, there may be a range of other concerns that are not immediately obvious in relation to aesthetic and affective judgements. For example, a study of English villagers' antipathy towards mobile telephone masts located in their village (Drake 2011) showed that the villagers were protesting not necessarily about the imputed health risks of the towers, which were disputed by the experts commenting on the issue, but the despoliation they perceived of their bucolic environment. Mobile phones and their associated masts were regarded as symbols of urban life, introducing values from the urban environment which the villagers regarded as incompatible with rural living. They were metaphorical pollutants, matter out of place, as Mary Douglas put it. However, the protesters did use health risks as a justification for their opposition, because of the power of scientific legitimacy such claims tend to carry in relation to concerns about aesthetics. Even these health claims were supported by the discourse of the rural environment as healthier than the urban environment. Such disputes bring to light the tensions within the neo-liberal concept of the concerned, entrepreneurial citizen. On the one hand, such ideal citizens are expected to control the risks to which they see themselves as being exposed and take steps to protect themselves against them. On the other, they are not encouraged to do so if they challenge state initiatives or market forces.

The above research emphasizes the importance of location or space in constructing concepts of risk. As writers in cultural geography have argued, space is an integral dimension of the affective dimension of risk. If a particular space feels forbidding to the people using it, fear and anxiety and a sense of being 'at risk' are evoked (Davidson and Milligan 2004). For example, the extensive fear of crime literature has placed some importance on the ways in which emotional responses such as fear of becoming a victim of crime are inspired by such features of the landscape as graffiti, broken windows and lack of street lighting and the design of buildings and public spaces. So too fear may be evoked by the presence of others in these spaces deemed threatening because of their behaviour or physical appearance, categorized as Other to Self. Public housing tower blocks, for example, may provoke fear from their residents because of their architectural features such as ground-floor pillars that potential criminals can hide behind, lack of fencing, poor lighting, non-existent security systems and dysfunctional locks on flats (Lees and Baxter 2011).

From this perspective, both the risk of crime and the fear of crime, and indeed, the notion of 'crime' itself, are dynamic, shifting assemblages that are constructed through social and cultural processes such as shared assumptions, localized circuits of knowledge and gossip, cultural mythologies, media representations and 'ways of seeing'. Thus, for example, a study of Australians living in rural areas found that they tended to conceptualize the risk of crime in relation to strangers from outside their areas. They perceived such newcomers as despoiling their rural idyll. They conceptualized newcomers as not part of their imagined sense of 'community' and thus as not 'fitting in', just as the English villagers in Drake's study discussed above viewed mobile phone towers as 'matter out of place'. The Australian rural dwellers also identified members of local socially and economically marginalized groups as representing a threat to their community because of their status as 'outsiders' (Scott *et al.* 2011).

It has been asserted that contradiction and contingency are more characteristic of contemporary reflexive subjectivity than is allowed by Beck and Giddens (Lash 1993, 2000). While both acknowledge the contingency inherent in 'risk society', particularly in relation to the incalculability of risk consequences and the changing state of expert knowledges, their focus on reflexivity tends to suggest that certainty is possible. Compulsive self-monitoring is not consistent with uncertainty and ambivalence, for these allow no guidelines by which self-monitoring can take place. Indeed, 'the very notion of "risk" entails making calculable the incalculable or the monitoring of contingency' (Lash 1993: 6). However, people often feel that knowledges about risk, including their own, are so precarious and contingent that they simply do not know which course of action to take. As a result, they may move between different risk positions at different times, sometimes attempting to control risk, at other times preferring a fatalistic approach that simply accepts the possibility of risk without attempting to avoid it.

The model of the rational actor, constantly calculating her or his exposure to a myriad of risks and then taking steps to diminish these risks, also tends to suggest that risk avoidance invariably takes place on a conscious level. This model assumes processes of human reasoning and behaviour that are based on calculation and economic rationality, with individuals represented as carefully weighing up the costs and benefits of various actions and making decisions based on these assessments (Bloor 1995: 92). Risk responses, however, need not necessarily take place on a conscious or 'rational' level. A distinction may be made between reflexive actions versus conventional or habitual actions which may be carried out without conscious deliberation. Such actions are products of acculturation which do not involve 'inner ethical problematization' but rather are acquired as 'a brute outcome of [individuals'] habitus or mode of life' (Hunter 1993: 128). Risk-related practices, therefore, may include both activities that may need high levels of problematization, the seeking out of advice or self-interrogation (should I do this or not?) but also those practices (perhaps better entitled 'habits') that do not involve such deliberation, but rather are experienced as 'second nature' to us (Binkley 2009).

Bourdieu's (1984) notion of the habitus is useful here to explore the habitual, acculturated nature of risk-related actions. The habitus is a set of dispositions and bodily techniques, modes of behaving and deporting oneself, that is passed on from generation to generation and is linked to membership of sub-cultural groups. These sets of dispositions and techniques are organizing principles by which sociocultural practices are maintained and reproduced. Style of dress, accent, way of walking, type of food eaten, the way one decorates one's home, the ways one spends one's leisure time, are all part of an individual's habitus, which are strongly influenced through notions of taste, style, pleasure and aesthetics. Most of the dispositions and behaviours that comprise an individual's habitus operate as habits, at the subconscious level. Indeed, the very difficulty of changing one's habits is founded on their almost automatic nature, their taken-for-granted participation in our mode of being and embodiment each day.

This perspective sees some aspects of risk avoidance as a part of everyday life that is often habitual, barely thought about because it has been adopted as part of people's every-day routines. Thus, for example, buckling up one's seat-belt each time one enters a car may well be a matter of habit for many people rather than a response to a feeling of concern or anxiety that is consciously recognized and dealt with on each occasion. So too, what may be labelled as 'risk-taking' activities in some discourses may instead be viewed by those who engage in them as part of everyday life and not as 'risks'. For instance, people who inject heroin are portrayed in public health discourses (and other sites, such as the mass media) as having lives characterized by the risk of injecting the drug, particularly in relation to contracting HIV and hepatitis. These 'risks' (as they were identified by others) may not be the only risk in these people's lives, or indeed, the most important risk from their perspective or even con-ceptualized as risky by them. In researching the everyday lived experiences of people using heroin in London, Rhodes observes that what is considered to be risk-taking behaviour from the perspective of public health tends to be merely rou-tine to the users: 'the act of injection, for established injectors, is situated within the world of the everyday. It is mundane and unspectacular. Preparing for an injection may become something akin to making breakfast or having a drink' (Rhodes 1995: 140). Here again, the disparities in how different groups of people conceptualize risk are evident.

Wilkinson (2006) points to the acute affective and embodied experiences of suffering, and the desire to avoid these, that underpin people's responses to risk. Rather than focusing on rational probabilistic thinking, he asserts, researchers interested in risk rationalities need to examine the cultural meanings related to the threat of suffering and previous experiences of suffering which underpin people's risk rationalities, whether it is poverty, unemployment, ill-health and disease, disability, pain, crime, violence, sexual abuse and so on. He notes that expert writing on risk tends to adopt a dispassionate tone, failing to convey the full affective meaning of the pain, fear, loss and suffering which underpin individuals' responses to risk.

One of the few academics in risk scholarship to have written about his own experiences of suffering in relation to his positioning as a 'risk victim' is John Tulloch (2006, 2008a, 2008b). Tulloch, who had published extensively on the sociological and cultural aspects of risk, was injured in the London bombing terrorist attack of 7 July 2005. He was travelling on a Tube train only about a metre away from one of the suicide bombers at the time the bomb was detonated. Tulloch subsequently found himself positioned as both a subject and object of risk discourse in relation to terrorism. He received a high level of media attention as one of the 'iconic images' of the bombing attacks, as one journalist described his photograph taken soon after they occurred.

This photograph appeared on the front pages of newspapers around the world (Tulloch, 2008b). In the image, Tulloch is shown standing outside Edgware Road Tube station looking distressed and dazed, his face covered in blood, a makeshift bandage around his head, his suit dirty and tattered.

Tulloch's insights into what he terms 'risk subjectivity', bringing together his lived experiences post the attack with his intellectual analysis of how he was constructed and positioned in media texts, provide insights into how 'risk victims' deal with everyday life, including fear of further dangers, the risk of continuing health problems and post-traumatic shock syndrome. Tulloch also describes how he attempted to resist the media's attempts to position him in certain ways. He was incensed when the photograph described above was used in the British *The Sun* newspaper two months after the attack to illustrate a front-page story on the Blair government's attempts to push through radical anti-terrorism legislation in Parliament. Tulloch's image was used next to a headline reading 'Tell Tony (Blair) he's right', suggesting that Tulloch agreed with this legislation and had been interviewed about it to provide comments for this news story. This was not the case: Tulloch had not been interviewed by *The Sun* and did not agree with Blair's legislation. He resented the new media's efforts to position him as a supporter of the British government's legislation and Britain's involvement in the Iraq War.

Tulloch argues that rather than scientific-expert discourses on risk being in opposition to subjective, lived experience-based discourses, they participate in a 'discursive co-construction' of both institutional and subjective risk rationalities. Tulloch found, for example, that scientific-expert knowledges on risk were helpful and empowering in his recovery from his injuries and the psychological trauma he suffered following the bombings. His own academic expert knowledge on the sociocultural and political dimensions of risk assisted his efforts to resist his positioning as a supporter of the Blair government's anti-terrorism proposals in the mass media. His embodied and affective experiences of everyday life post the attacks have contributed to the knowledges he developed from scientific and expert risk discourses. The governmentality approach's emphasis on the operation of power from above is challenged by analyses such as Tulloch's, which are able to demonstrate that risk subjectivities are constructed using both everyday, embodied vernacular understandings of risk and technico-scientific definitions.

CONCLUDING COMMENTS

This chapter has developed a viewpoint on lay actors' responses to risk that recognizes the importance of reflexivity in relation to risk in the context of late modernity. However, it goes beyond what is seen to be a limited notion of reflexivity as represented in the work of such writers as Giddens and Beck in acknowledging that reflexivity involves not simply rational, individualistic assessment of expert knowledges but also the development of knowledge based on everyday experience and relationships with other lay actors. Further, reflexivity is not simply based on cognitive judgements but is also founded in aesthetic, affective or hermeneutic judgements that are developed through acculturation.

People may respond habitually to risk, which means that they do not consciously weigh up risks and benefits but rather include risk avoidance as part of the habits of their everyday lives. Risk responses are also developed via people's membership of social groups and networks, their access to material resources and their location within the life course and relations of power. These are aspects which shape the capacity of individuals to comport themselves as the ideal autonomous citizen that is expected of them in risk-related discourses.

The importance of acknowledging the shared and symbolic meanings of risk has again been highlighted in this chapter. The next chapter addresses these aspects of risk in greater detail, by exploring the ways in which notions of Otherness constantly emerge in individuals' and social groups' responses to risk.

7

RISK AND OTHERNESS

As observed in earlier chapters, many theoretical discussions of risk tend not to acknowledge the differentiation of the targeting and effects of risk discourses on specific social groups. They represent the risk actor, in many cases, as lacking a gender, age, ethnicity, social class, geographical location or sexual identity. Statements about risk and subjectivity tend to elide differences, presenting the risk subject as universal. As noted in Chapter 4, Beck has claimed in his writings on world risk society and cosmopolitanism that distinctions between Self and Other are breaking down as nation-states have been forced to cooperate with each other. A close examination of the ways in which risk discourses operate as strategies of normalization, of exclusion and inclusion, however, demonstrates that in most cases notions of Otherness – and the consequent stigmatizing and marginalizing of the Other – remain central to ways of thinking and acting about risk.

The 'cultural/symbolic' approach, in its focus on risk and Otherness, goes some way to emphasize that fears about risk tend to be projected onto certain social groups: those that are defined as the dangerous 'risky' Other, requiring control and intervention. As Mary Douglas' writings have shown, the Other – that which is conceptualized as radically different from Self – is the subject of anxiety and concern, particularly if it threatens to blur boundaries, to overtake the Self. These anxieties and fears tend to emerge from and cohere around the body, which itself is a highly potent symbolic object. This chapter begins with a discussion of how Otherness is conceptualized, followed by an analysis of the links between dominant notions of the body and concerns about risk and Otherness. We then explore accounts of the ambivalence produced by hybridity and liminality and the psychoanalytic dimension of responses to Otherness, particularly in relation to the abject. The chapter ends with a discussion of spatiality as it relates to questions of risk and the Other.

CONCEPTUALIZING OTHERNESS

Otherness, as discussed in Chapter 3, is a product of observations of difference/strangeness. Otherness is dangerous because it confounds order and control: 'Encountering the other is to expose oneself to the abyss of difference ... difference which attracts us precisely because of the richness it contains, but which is also fraught with risk and instant danger' (Melucci 1996: 101). The Other represents the unknown and the threat of loss of one's own identity through contact with this unknown, the dissipation of boundaries and the realization of our own limits: 'encountering another always entails putting into question something of ourselves and of our uniqueness and venturing into an unknown land only to discover what we lack' (ibid.: 101).

Otherness involves not only that which is placed directly in opposition to the Self/Us, as part of a binary opposition, but also that which is uncertain, confusing and blurs the ordering of binary oppositions – the hybrid and the liminal. As Douglas argued (Chapter 3), that which is seen to be anomalous, difficult to classify, creates feelings of unease and repulsion. Bauman (1991) has also written about the 'acute discomfort' and anxiety we feel about ambivalence, when we are able to assign an object or event to more than one category. As he notes: 'To classify ... is to give the world a *structure*: to manipulate its probabilities; to make some events more likely than some others; to behave as if events were not random, or to limit or eliminate randomness of events' (ibid.: 1, original emphasis). In classifying, we perform acts of inclusion and exclusion. Ordering is the central task of modernity, an attempt to fend off chaos. The imperative of reason in modernity has led to intolerance of things that cannot readily be ordered and categorized: 'The other of order is the miasma of the indeterminate and unpredictable. The other is the uncertainty, that source and archetype of all fear' (ibid.: 7).

The use of dichotomies as a separation practice is central to ordering. The Other or opposite is the 'degraded, suppressed, exiled' side of the first member of the opposition (Bauman 1991: 14). Bauman gives the example of 'nature', positioned as Other to science and to humanity in post-Enlightenment thought. Modern science 'was born out of the overwhelming ambition to conquer Nature and subordinate it to human needs' (ibid.: 39). Nature was designated as anything that spoilt order, harmony or design and thus refused purpose or meaning: rivers that flow in the wrong direction, plants that seed themselves where they spoil the harmony of arrangements of flora, animals that are not useful to humans. Bauman identifies this thinking about science and nature in Nazi ideas about the importance of 'racial hygiene', underlying the impetus of the Holocaust. The Jews were represented in Nazi writings as dirty, unhygienic, pathological, contaminating, literally as 'vermin' and therefore requiring 'extermination' in the interests of cleanliness and hygiene:

> Defining the Other as vermin harnesses the deeply entrenched fears, revulsion and disgust in the service of extermination. But also, and more seminally, it places the Other at an enormous mental distance at which moral rights are no longer visible. Having been stripped of humanity and redefined as vermin, the Other is no more an object of moral evaluation.
>
> (Bauman 1991: 48)

Portraying certain social groups as more animal than human has served to represent them as the dangerous Other because of their supposed lack of humanity. Non-white peoples have frequently been portrayed as animalistic by bourgeois northern Europeans, as have such minority groups as the working class, the Gypsies, the Irish and the Jews (Sibley 1995: 26–8). In the history of European writings on race, particularly in the colonial era, black people have been constantly singled out as Other: as uncivilized, uncontrolled, irrational, dirty, diseased and therefore threatening to white people and their purity (ibid.: 19–24).

A contemporary analysis of American neighbourhoods and how certain individuals and social groups are defined as 'Other' points to the ways in which exclusionary categories are maintained and reproduced as part of everyday life (Perin 1988). The kinds of lines or boundaries that are routinely drawn in this sociocultural context include those

> between business and pleasure, home and work, relatives and friends, between the things we do for love and those we do for money, between what is private and public, between good and evil ... and, as well, those between family and community, between the genders, between the species, between adults and children, between the races, between body and spirit, even between city and suburb.
>
> (Perin 1988: 4)

It is when 'lines do not hold', when ambiguities and subsequent confusion appear to flourish, that the 'most socially divisive, destructive, and estranging impulses can be revealed' (Perin 1988: 4). It is here that the Other is identified, marginalized and often stigmatized as potentially dangerous, dirty or defiling.

EMBODIMENT AND OTHERNESS

Concepts of embodiment are central to those of Otherness. The ideal notion of the human body in contemporary Western societies is that of a body which is tight, contained, exercising full control over its boundaries and what comes inside and goes outside. At its most extreme, this ideal seeks to disallow the very existence of the material body, seeking the perfection and purity of rational thought over the impurities of fleshly desires and needs. Many of the 'risks' identified in past eras and in the present are seen to directly threaten the integrity or health of one's body. As Douglas' work has shown, notions of risk often use the fleshly body as a symbol for the body politic. Symbolic meanings, however, are also directly applied to material bodily practices.

Across historical eras and sociocultural contexts, a range of bodily practices that have been established to deal with risk may be identified. Changing notions of the body over the centuries in Western societies have been accompanied by changes in the ways in which risk has been conceptualized and dealt with. In particular, the notion of the 'open' body that dominated in antiquity and the medieval era in Europe has gradually been replaced by that of the ideal of the 'closed' body, emergent in early modernity and becoming dominant in the contemporary era. Each model of the body has implications for risk epistemologies and concepts of Otherness.

In the pre-modern era, the body was thought of as a microcosm, an open world which embraced forces that gushed forth through the orifices of the lower body. The 'higher' regions of the body (the head/mind/soul) were privileged as nobler than the 'lower' regions, which were considered to be the sites of generation and decay. The medieval body, however, remained a largely uncontrolled, sensuous and volatile body, open to the world. The body was seen as part of a communal whole, freely interacting with others' bodies. Since the body was thought of as open, it was conceptualized as constantly susceptible to invasion. While there were many fears and uncertainties relating to the body, these were linked largely with magic and the supernatural, those phenomena thought of as beyond human control such as demons and evil spirits (Elias 1939/1994; Bakhtin 1984; Muchembled 1985; Ferguson 1997). To deal with the threat of invasion of the body by such sinister forces, causing illness and death, a range of taboos and protective rites were established to police the body's openings and protect it (Muchembled 1985; Ferguson 1997). Urine was particularly potent, seen as bearing the essence of a person, and as a conduit between inside and outside the body. It was thought, for example, that urinating against the same wall upon which a leper had also urinated could result in contracting leprosy oneself (Muchembled 1985: 72). The open body, however, was also celebrated, particularly in carnivalesque rituals, in which the 'grotesque' nature of the open body, its excessive physicality, was a source of revelry and pleasure (Bakhtin 1984; Ferguson 1997).

The emergence of the ideal of the 'closed' body in early modernity led to a change in ways of thinking about contamination and purity. A division between the fleshly body and the non-material spirit emerged, with the body more negatively identified with the 'flesh' 'as a helpless and inherently corruptible creature' (Ferguson 1997: 19), thus requiring continual denial and discipline by the will (Ferguson 1997; Mellor and Shilling 1997). The inside of the body was conceptualized as disorderly, dangerous and ugly, compared with the outside of the body. The ideal body was represented as noble, the key to human progress through self-contemplation and the insights of the senses. This body was autonomous, individuated and closed off from other bodies. In the early modern era, the body, which was previously subject to external regulation, became viewed as principally self-regulated through rational thought and action. The ideal of self-discipline of the body became privileged in relation to what went in and out of the body and how the body was comported. This was accompanied by a network of regulations concerning the management and control of the body (Elias 1939/1994).

The progressive change from the open, 'grotesque' body to the closed or 'civilized' body (Elias 1939/1994) resulted in the intensification of anxieties about the orifices of the body and what flows in and out of it. When the body was conceptualized as open to the world, as inevitably porous and only weakly subject to the control of the individual, pleasure as well as fear accompanied the flow of forces in and out of the body. The increasing emphasis on self-regulation, the closing off of the body as much as possible, resulted in greater anxiety about the possibility of loss of self-control and the blurring of boundaries between inside and outside, and Self and Other. By the nineteenth century, the 'grotesque' body – that which was seen to be unable to control its bodily boundaries – was greeted with disgust and horror, particularly on the part of the ruling and bourgeois classes (Stallybrass and White 1986).

In the late modern era, particularly in Anglophone and northern European societies, it is considered extremely important in most cases to maintain a distinction from others' bodies, to tightly shut one's body off. With an intense focus on the social importance of maintaining and presenting a 'civilized' body, there is evidence of a high level of concern and anxiety around manifold issues to do with body boundaries, including the fluids that flow in and out of the body, the ways in which others touch one's body and the deportment and appearance of the body. Apart from a very small number of intimates, those who are seen to get too close to one's body are perceived as dangerous, alarming and threatening (Grosz 1994; Miller 1997).

Parts of one's own body, such as the genitals and anus, also evoke fear, anxiety and disgust because they are culturally coded as contaminating and dirty, and therefore as highly risky to touch, by oneself or others. As a result, 'We can become the other to ourselves and engage in various forms of disgusting behaviour that are understood as violations of the self' (Miller 1997: 51). What we find disgusting is that which is seen to impose a threat of some sort to our bodily or self-integrity. Central to our feeling of disgust is our sense that boundaries have been transgressed. Such substances as chewed food that has been spat out and vomit are found to be revolting and contaminating because they flout the rule that 'what goes in to the body should not come out again'. Substances that originate from within the body and emit from bodily orifices (the nose, the eyes, the genitals, the anus, the mouth) are risky and potentially defiling to oneself and others when they escape from the proper place – inside the body – to outside the body and we are made aware of their existence (Miller 1997; McGinn 2011). Except in very special cases (such as consensual sexual intercourse, medical encounters and carers dealing with the bodily fluids of infants and young children), contact with bodily substances deemed to be contaminating or having one's bodily orifices penetrated by the bodily parts or bodily substances of others tends to invoke a host of strong emotions, including fear, anger, revulsion, horror, disgust and anxiety. These emotions may be produced not only in relation to one's own body but also to those bodies with whom one has an intimate relationship.

The term 'panic bodies' (Kroker and Kroker 1988) has been used to describe the emotions that people feel about their bodies and the threat of penetration by a range of phenomena that are currently deemed to be malign, such as viruses and bacteria, pollutants, food, drugs and other people's bodily fluids. It has been argued that the diffuse anxieties individuals feel about the apparent breakdown of traditions in late modern society are worked out on their bodies, in their intense concerns about protecting their body boundaries from invasion and dissipation. Kroker and Kroker describe this phenomenon as 'Body McCarthyism', 'which insists on the (unattainable) ideal of absolute purity of the body's circulatory exchanges as the new gold standard of an immunological polities' (ibid.: 11). In this new politics, hygienic standards come to stand for ways of identifying Self and Other, with the Other standing as the contaminated, polluting threat to the purity of Self.

The white, able-bodied, bourgeois, heterosexual masculine body is valued as most closely conforming to this idea of the contained, 'civilized' body, while the bodies of women, the working class, non-whites, the disabled and gay men are set apart as the Other, for they are represented as incapable of fully achieving the mastery of the body. Such bodies are culturally represented as subject to the will of the flesh rather than that of reason, prone to emotionality, excessive desire, violence or disarray (Grosz 1994; Lupton 1995; Sibley 1995; Shildrick 2007).

Women have traditionally been considered closer to 'nature' and the 'body', while men have been constantly associated with 'culture' and the 'mind'. Women have been constantly represented in Western societies as less capable of physical and emotional control, supposedly ruled by their hormones and reproductive organs. The pregnant woman, the post-partum woman, the menstruating woman and the sexually aroused or seductive woman are treated in a wide range of cultures as transgressive, polluting, risky figures. Their bodies are represented as open to the world, as fluid and leaky, incapable of regulation, escaping and evading the boundaries of the clean and the proper (Kristeva 1982; Grosz 1994).

Similarly, non-white people have traditionally been represented as lacking the capacity for 'civilized' containment of their bodies. Nineteenth-century British colonialist and medical discourses in South Africa, for example, portrayed black Africans as inherently dirty and diseased, as 'savage' rather than 'civilized', as both morally and physically degenerate. In describing black Africans as 'dirty' and 'greasy', the British portrayed the black body as porous, odorous and damp, and therefore as potentially contaminating to those who came into contact with it, in stark contrast to the ideal of the white European as clean, contained and controlled (Comaroff 1993).

Gypsies and other Travellers and nomads are traditionally considered Other and therefore threatening and risky because of their peripatetic habits and their lack of adherence to usual norms of the settled world. These groups are simultaneously viewed as romantic, alluring and exotic, but are also positioned as dirty, lacking personal hygiene and unable to properly control their body boundaries, encroaching on and despoiling other people's land or public spaces, lacking appropriate morals and thus prone to sexual promiscuity and petty crime such as theft. Their lack of a settled home and region has resulted in nomadic groups being viewed by others as backward, animalistic, parasitic upon others and uncivilized, and thus subject to suspicion, disgust and stigmatization (Wild 2005).

People with a disability, because they fail to conform to standards of 'normality' as they are espoused in a culture, are also often treated as sub-human and subjected to fear, disgust, anger and abuse (Thomson 1997; Shildrick 2007). The category of the 'physically disabled' is produced by legal, medical, political, cultural and literary narratives that comprise an exclusionary discourse, constructing the bodies of members of this category as insufficient and deviant. They thus become a repository for social anxieties about vulnerability, control and identity: 'the disabled figure operates as the vividly embodied, stigmatized other whose social role is to symbolically free the privileged, idealized figure of the American self from the vagaries and vulnerabilities of embodiment' (Thomson 1997: 7). Here again Douglas' notion of dirt as anomalous and extraordinary may be used to argue that disabled bodies are conceptualized, like dirt, as lying outside the normative ordering system of Western societies. Like dirt, people categorized as disabled have been dealt with through policies of policing, regulation, exclusion and avoidance in the effort to re-establish sociocultural order.

HYBRIDITY AND LIMINALITY

The hybrid is that which combines two types thought of as distinct from each other in such a way as to merge their characteristics into a new type, or the separation of a single entity into two or more parts, rendering each different from the other (Young 1995: 26). It has been argued by some commentators that the globalizing processes of late modernity are producing new and transitional forms of hybrid identities. These identities confound, confuse and challenge established ideas about the distinctions between different types of cultural identity. Hybrid identities are constantly in flux, remaking boundaries rather than bolstering them. As a result, 'difference is neither One nor the Other, but *something else besides, in-between*' (Bhabha 1994: 219, original emphasis). The fluid, contingent nature of identities, the requirement that they must be actively performed, means that they are never finished, complete. It is in the interstices of binary oppositions and definitions of identity that hybridity is generated and flourishes. Hybridity is always risky, however, because of its unbounded nature, its defiance of taken-for-granted categories.

Hybridity has long been the cause of great concern and anxiety among privileged groups who are threatened by the idea of their gene stock or 'blood', for example, being adulterated and contaminated by mixing with other races. Such a mixing was believed to produce a hybrid stock that was weak and degenerate, less civilized than the Aryan race. This anxiety was particularly dominant in the nineteenth century, a time in which colonialism involved the movement of Europeans into other continents peopled by races deemed by them to be inferior and animalistic. At the heart of racial theory espoused in the Victorian era in England, for example, was evidence of an obsession and fascination with issues of sexuality between members of different races, fertility, miscegenation and interracial transgression (Young 1995). Voyeuristic tableaux of 'frenzied, interminable copulation, of couplings, fusing, coalescence ... this steamy model of mixture' (ibid.: 181) between races appeared again and again in the nineteenth-century literature of racial theories.

In a history of Vancouver's Chinatown area, it is observed that this space was set apart in mainstream discourses in the nineteenth and early twentieth centuries as a site of vice, disease, danger and corruption because of the presence of Chinese people (Anderson 1996). Like the Orient of Western imagining described by Edward Said in his influential *Orientalism* (1978), Vancouver's Chinatown served as the place of the Other for the majority white population, helping it forge its own understanding of identity and cultural boundaries. There was a particular concern on the part of bourgeois whites about the sexual interaction of Chinese and white people, not only in relation to sexually transmitted diseases that the Chinese were believed to harbour but also to the threat of contamination of the white population of Canada through the production of mixed race 'stock' or the 'mongrelization' of white 'purity'. In visual and verbal representations, the Chinese were portrayed as flooding into Canada, as an 'influx' threatening to sweep away the dominance of whites and overcome them through sheer force of numbers. Canadian white family life was set up in opposition to and at risk from the corruption of the Chinese. White women in particular were positioned as being at risk from the sexual desires of the lascivious, exotic Oriental man (Anderson 1996).

The liminal is that which represents a transitional, middle stage between two distinctly different entities, identities or sites. It thus cannot be categorized into either: it is 'in-between'.

In contemporary Western societies, bodies that are seen to transgress or blur culturally important boundaries are the source of confusion, fear, anxiety and even hatred, revulsion and disgust. The blurring of the binary opposition between male and female, for example, inspires strong emotions. Such figures as gay men and lesbians, transsexuals and transvestites, highly-muscled female bodybuilders, men in drag and those rare cases of individuals who are born with ambiguous genitalia are continually subjected to negative reactions because of the challenge they pose to the taken-for-granted major distinctions between male and female identity.

Liminal figures, such as the stranger who crosses borders between 'inside' and 'outside' a social group, are commonly treated as threats to social order. The figure of 'the stranger' is a central source of uncertainty in late modern societies. We observed in Chapter 6 that the figure of the stranger or the outsider often evokes fear and a sense of being threatened. Strangers are deemed threatening because of their behaviour or physical appearance, categorized as Other to Self. They are unknown, and therefore unknowable and unpredictable. The stranger cannot yet be categorized as either friend or enemy and is therefore disorderly, blurring boundaries and division. The ambivalence created by strangers' liminal status, their monstrous status as neither–nor, creates uncertainty, which at best is discomforting and at worst carries a sense of danger. 'Undecidables' such as strangers paralyze knowledge and action: 'They bring the outside into the inside, and poison the comfort of order with suspicion of chaos' (Bauman 1991: 56).

Bauman takes up Douglas's discussion of the horror produced by the slimy (see Chapter 3) in using the term 'sliminess' to describe the indeterminate nature of neither–nor figures such as strangers, which blur 'a boundary line vital to the construction of a particular social order or a particular life-world' (Bauman 1991: 61). He notes that the 'stranger' and other marginal figures are dealt with in two major ways by societies. One strategy is 'anthropophagic', involving 'annihilating strangers by devouring them and then metabolically transforming them into a tissue indistinguishable from one's own' (Bauman 1995: 2). The other strategy is 'anthropoemic', involving 'vomiting the strangers, banishing them from the limits of the orderly world and barring them from all communication with those inside' (ibid.: 2).

Encounters with homeless people confront individuals with deeply felt anxieties about the rational ordering of society and of individuals (Mossman 1997; Casey *et al.* 2008). Homeless people tend to be placed conceptually in that category usually reserved for animals. This is because the distinction between 'nature' (or the animal world) and 'culture' (the human world) rests upon such differences as animals have no permanent homes, live outdoors, roam about, void their wastes outside, do not wash, smell offensive and have little control over their actions, while humans dwell in fixed residences, void their body wastes privately and indoors, bathe and use deodorant to avoid smelling badly, and exert control over their actions. In a liminal conceptual space between these categories are pet animals (who have become partly humanized through such actions as allowing them in the house and providing them with names) and homeless people. The latter are conceptualized as partly animalistic because although they are biologically human, they do not fit the distinctions between 'animal' and 'human'. Homeless people may even be conceptualized as 'dirt', as matter out of place that requires removal so as to regain order and purity. Their liminal status means that they can be treated more harshly and as having fewer rights than other people, including confining them involuntarily to institutions.

Animals too, have become increasingly portrayed as the dangerous Other in risk discourses. Such crises as 'mad cow' disease, dioxin in chickens, salmonella in eggs and trans-species viral infections that have caused pandemics such as the avian and swine flus, as well as news media reports of wild or domesticated animals that have attacked humans, have positioned animals as the source of illness, injury, infection and death. Media coverage of these animal-related risks has raised the spectre of savage, diseased or mutated species created by humans' meddling with 'natural' processes. Such portrayals reflect the ambivalence felt by humans towards nature. Nature is positioned in some representations as the superior, pure Other to the Self of humanity, but in others as contaminated, wild, out-of-control and highly dangerous to human health and well-being (Washer 2006; Nerlich and Halliday 2007; Gerber *et al.* 2011). These dangerous animals are positioned in some cases as liminal, such as domesticated dogs that seem almost human-like but which then may turn on humans and attack them, and hybrid, such as 'mad cows' that have consumed other animals' remains and thus been transformed by human action from herbivores to carnivores, or trans-species viruses that are able to cross between humans and other animal species.

All these commentaries point to the importance of order and control in the late modern sensibility, and the emphasis that is placed on categorization and keeping things in their 'proper' conceptual place. Those things that are not easily categorized, that fail to stay in their categories, or that simply are too different from the Self, tend to arouse anxieties and fears. They are culturally designated as potentially polluting and contaminating to Self, and as a result, are typically dealt with using exclusionary tactics that seek to locate them as far as possible, both symbolically and literally, from the Self.

THE PSYCHODYNAMICS OF OTHERNESS

A further perspective on Otherness is articulated in psycho-analytic theory, which focuses on the projection of uncon-scious emotions and fantasies upon the Other as part of individuals' continuing attempts to maintain a coherent and untroubled subjectivity and to construct and maintain con-ceptual borders. When 'badness' is projected onto the Other, this works to maintain the concept of the 'good Self' by splitting off those unconscious feelings of badness and locat-ing them elsewhere (Kent 2001; Hier 2004; Salter and Mutlu 2011).

Julia Kristeva (1982) has drawn upon both Douglas' the-orizing of pollution beliefs and psychoanalytic theory, par-ticularly that of object relations theory, to construct an argument looking at the ambivalent notion of the 'abject'. Object relations theory, as it has been presented in the work of writers such as Klein and Winnicott, examines the psy-chodynamics of the young child's individuation from the mother figure. It is argued that in infancy, the child experi-ences the body and Self as joined with that of the mother – there is no distinct boundary between Self and Other, subject and object. As part of cognitive and emotional development, the child gradually comes to recognize that its body is separate from that of the mother. This realization is accompanied by feelings of terror, anger, insecurity, loss and grief, as well as desire to achieve oneness again with the mother's body.

Those who have adopted object-relations theory contend that the ontological state of selfhood, therefore, is a process that is constantly in tension with an individual's relationship with another: first, the mother's body/self, but later other objects (people, things, emotions). Through gradual acculturation as infants into the social world, we define our selves and demarcate our boundaries of selfhood and embodiment against that which is not us, which is Other:

> The sense of border which emerges in infancy is not an innate sense but a consequence of relating to others and becoming a part of a culture. Thus, the boundary between the inner (pure) self and the outer (defiled) self, which is initially manifest in a distaste for bodily residues but then assumes a much wider cultural significance, derives from parents and other adults who are, by definition, socialized and acculturated.
>
> (Sibley 1995: 7)

Into adulthood, the feelings that accompanied our loss of the mother continue to be experienced as part of our relations with objects, which become invested with these feelings as they are split off from the Self as a defence mechanism. Some objects become the repositories of very negative feelings: hate, anger, frustration, revulsion, disgust. Others become objects of our love and desire. Some are both simultaneously. That which we most fear, which we construct as the Other, is also often that which we most desire. For Kristeva (1982), this Other is the abject, the source of endless fascination as well as horror, which disturbs identity, boundaries and order, from which we continually seek to escape but yet are drawn to and inextricably linked to. Abjection, she argues, is a powerful feeling which is both symbolic and experienced as a bodily sensation. Above all, abjection is 'a revolt of the person against an external menace from which one wants to keep oneself at a distance' (ibid.: 135). Kristeva describes the emotional and bodily responses that the abject incurs – loathing, spasms, vomiting, repugnance, retching – as a means of 'protection' from the Other.

The abject is viewed as dirty, filthy, contaminating and waste, that which confounds boundaries. As Kristeva notes: 'It is thus not lack of cleanliness or health that causes abjection but what disturbs identity, system, order. What does not respect borders, positions, rules. The in-between, the ambiguous, the composite' (1982: 4). The abject, thus, is not fully Other because its boundaries continually threaten to merge with our own, and this is what renders it so threatening. The abject is always inherent within the self even though we seek constantly to expel it from our selves so as to render our selves pure and bounded: 'It is something rejected from which one does not part, from which one does not protect oneself as from an object. Imaginary uncanniness and real threat, it beckons to us and ends up engulfing us' (ibid.: 4). Rituals directed at maintaining boundaries between Self and Other, the subject and the object, are thus attempts to ward off abjection by establishing separation, maintaining one's own body as 'clean and proper'. These goals are never fully achieved, for purity is only ever an optimum goal to aim for – it can never be fully accomplished.

The notion of the abject, as a psychodynamic phenomenon that is constructed through social and cultural processes but is experienced as a series of emotions arising from within, provides some explanation for the 'irrational' virulent feelings to which some individuals and social groups are exposed. One example is fat people, who historically have been routinely constructed as uncontained, excessive and unregulated, lacking the self-control necessary to keep their bodies tightly disciplined. More than this, an integral dimension of the ways in which fat people are culturally portrayed and treated is with disgust and revulsion (Lupton 2012c). The constant association of fatness with disease and ill health results in the fat body bearing the negative meanings of illness and death. Fat people have become the repository of fears and anxieties about the death, illness, chaos, lack of control and the incipient permeability of the social and fleshly body. The uncontained nature of the fat body, its looseness and liquidity, its lack of defined boundaries and tendency to ooze, inspires abjection. The abject fat body inspires a desire to distance oneself from it and also to prevent one's own body becoming similarly abject. Attempts to reduce the size of the fat body via dieting, exercise, drugs or weight surgery, therefore, may be conceptualized as efforts to counter the abjection of the fat of the body within oneself, to expel it (Kent 2001).

Kristeva identifies the corpse as a primary figure of abjection, because of its in-between role between humanity and organic matter: 'A decaying body, lifeless, completely turned into dejection, blurred between the inanimate and the inorganic ... the corpse represents fundamental pollution' (1982: 4). Other figures who are routinely culturally defined as abject are those individuals who are hypocritical, who flout the moral order: the 'traitor, the liar, the criminal with a good conscience, the shameless rapist, the killer who claims he is a saviour' (ibid.: 4). For Kristeva, however, it is the figure of the woman's body that is most likely to be positioned as abject, because of the psychodynamic struggles that occur during individuation, when the child must separate its body and identity from that of the mother. This process of individuation, she argues, 'is a violent, clumsy breaking away, with the constant risk of falling back under the sway of a power as securing as it is stifling' (ibid.: 13). It can only take place by rendering the mother's body as abject, rejecting it and repelling it.

Because of this process of abjection via individuation, women in general tend to be positioned as Other, as transgressors of the proper. Elizabeth Grosz has taken up Douglas' and Kristeva's discussion to analyse the symbolic nature of sexual bodily fluids, with a particular focus on gender implications. I have earlier referred to the symbolic contaminating nature of bodily fluids in general when they escape the body, going from 'inside' to 'outside'. The female body is conceptualized as more marginal, indeterminate, fluid, borderline and liminal than the male body, as seeping sexual fluids such as menstrual blood that are considered to be particularly 'dirty' because of their provenance (the mysterious uterus and hidden female genitals). The female body tends therefore to be viewed as more dangerous, defiling and diseased than the male body:

> It is not the case that men's bodily fluids are regarded as polluting and contaminating for women in the same way or to the same extent as women's are for men. It is women and what men consider to be their inherent capacity for contagion, their draining, demanding bodily processes that have figured so strongly in cultural representations, and that have emerged so clearly as a problem for social control.
>
> (Grosz 1994: 197)

As a consequence of this cultural coding, in discourses on sexually transmissible diseases, for example, heterosexual women are represented as more potentially contaminating than are heterosexual men and the burden of responsibility is placed upon them to protect both themselves and their male sexual partners from infection. Women's fluid and open bodies, and particularly their sexual organs, are constructed as repositories of contamination. Because men's bodies are seen to be more contained, closed off from the world, they are represented as less contaminating, more 'at risk' from women than as posing a risk to their partners (Grosz 1994: 197).

To summarize, as part of the psychodynamics of constructing and maintaining boundaries of selfhood, other individuals and objects are invested with emotion, both positive and negative. Those individuals who are defined as 'dirty', as 'matter out of place' and as abject, are positioned in the unconscious as the 'bad object', marginalized beyond the boundaries of acceptable Self. The emotions of fear, anxiety and loathing are projected onto them, as they become the repositories for that which members of the dominant group hate and fear within themselves.

SPATIALITY AND OTHERNESS

Knowledge and meaning, as cultural geographers emphasize, are inevitably spatially as well as socially, politically and historically situated. Spatial metaphors and binary oppositions are central in notions of Self and Other. When we refer to the boundaries of the body/society, to the distinction between inside and outside, to the marginalized or excluded, we are relying on spatial metaphors and binary oppositions. Notions of space themselves are cultural objects, constructed through social, political and historical processes. But the importance of space and place in relation to concepts of riskiness lies not simply in their value as metaphor, but in their materiality. The members of 'risky' marginalized groups are viewed by the dominant group as polluting public spaces, and they shrink from contact, physical or otherwise, with them. Strategies of exclusion directed at 'risky' individuals or sub-groups are often explicitly concerned with maintaining bodies within certain geographical limits: 'The human landscape can be read as a landscape of exclusion' (Sibley 1995: ix).

In Western societies there are many strategies directed at policing public spaces and attempting to remove members of threatening marginalized groups from areas designated as appropriate only for the privileged. Such spatial binary oppositions as high/low have often served to organize these strategies. Stallybrass and White (1986) have examined the high/low binary opposition as it appears and is acted upon in four symbolic domains: psychic forms, the human body, geographical space and the social order. As they note, the high/low opposition 'is a fundamental basis to mechanisms of ordering and sense-making in European cultures' (ibid.: 3). What is coded as the 'low' bears particular weight in terms of the contradictory and ambivalent emotions it evokes, including both revulsion and desire, repugnance and fascination. A recurrent pattern emerges in which the 'top' attempts to reject and eliminate the 'bottom' to preserve order and prestige. But through these processes of rejection and exclusion, the 'top' discovers a dependence on this Other and the low is symbolically reincorporated into its fantasy life. It is therefore not simply a matter of the opposition between high and low being rigidly maintained as a practice of exclusion. Paradoxically exclusion breeds further incorporation: the repressed continually returns.

As was noted earlier in this chapter, for the bourgeoisie in early modern Europe, the open or 'grotesque' body became disavowed, removed from the Self and projected onto Others. Indeed, according to Stallybrass and White (1986: Chapter 3), the bourgeois public sphere became dependent on denial of the grotesque, the irrational, the bodily. In the nineteenth century the city became a focus of the bourgeoisie's anxiety about contamination and disorder, via a concern about the sewer and the slums and the figures of the prostitute, the servant, the labourer, the scavenger, the beggar and the criminal. 'As the bourgeoisie produced new forms of regulation and prohibition governing their own bodies, they wrote ever more loquaciously of the body of the Other – of the city's "scum"' (ibid.: 126). The bourgeoisie's concerns about maintaining the propriety and cleanliness of the body, to disavow the presence of the 'lower' body and its functions, were mirrored in their concerns with the city and its lower strata. The working class and the poor, the people who lived and worked on the streets, were viewed as transgressing the boundary separating human from animal in their contact with dirt and disease, their degraded living conditions and their lack of bodily control. New forms of surveillance and discipline were developed in the attempt to control these contaminating bodies, including bodily regimes around cleanliness, dress, diet and deportment. Plans attempting to control the built environment of the city were developed and implemented so that working-class housing and slums would be kept apart from the eyes and noses of the bourgeoisie.

In contemporary Western societies, the figure of the criminal is frequently positioned as risky and requiring exclusion from others. As part of the strategy of dealing with the risk and uncertainty of crime, people develop a 'mental map' of places, defining some as likely to be 'safe' and others as 'risky'. This 'mental map' does not simply rely on geographical aspects of a space or place, but also draws on ideas and assumptions about social relations and the kinds of people who inhabit or pass through these spaces and places at specific times of day and night. Fear of crime tends to be located within public rather than private space, as the criminal is considered to be an 'unpredictable stranger' rather than someone known to oneself, and thus as inhabiting public space rather than being encountered in one's home. Members of such social groups as young working-class men, the unemployed and injecting drug users are typically nominated as potential criminals because of their assumed simmering resentments against society and lack of capacity for self-control. Those spaces in which they move about – the inner city, the shopping mall, the housing estate – are considered 'dangerous' in terms of the risk of crime and therefore as requiring increased surveillance, police presence and caution on the part of those who traverse them (Lupton 1999).

Since the early 1990s surveillance technologies such as closed circuit television (CCTV) and biometric identity documents for use in traversing national borders have increasingly been deployed in the attempt to monitor and protect public spaces, particularly those deemed 'risky spaces' because of those individuals who move through them (Hier 2004; Salter and Mutlu 2011). Such technologies involve not only social monitoring but also social exclusion of individuals considered to be undesirable, posing a threat in some way. These people tend to belong to defined social groups: young people (particularly young men), homeless people, street traders and black men (Hier 2004). In the wake of 11 September 2001, men of a Middle Eastern appearance have also been singled out for special surveillance, particularly at airports and in border surveillance. It has been argued that such measures are a way of dealing with the fear, anxiety, panic and trauma that events such as those on 11 September 2001 and 7 July 2005 have incited. National border security controls are a means of providing a figurative as well as literal barrier between the threatening Others and Us at a time at which terrorist attacks have rent open notions of containment between inside and outside. These measures are never able to fully control the unexpected or guarantee improved security, but they function at an unconscious level to help reassert feelings of safety and security (Salter and Mutlu 2011).

Strategies of exclusion exerted on the part of the most powerful in a society in their attempts to avoid risk often serve to incite fear and anxiety in those they seek to exclude or intimidate. The bodies of white, heterosexual, bourgeois men tend to claim public space as a right, and frequently seek to dominate and exclude others through exerting an aggressive gaze or through violence. Other bodies must fight to establish their place in this space. Feminists have written about the ways in which women, as one of the Other categories of bodies within public spaces, are positioned as vulnerable to confrontation or attack and therefore tend to lack the self-possession of privileged men in the same space. Moving in public space, for women, is constantly problematic, making them feel uneasy or anxious, exposed to the gaze, evaluation and imminent threat of (masculine) others (Lupton 1999; Whitzman 2007).

Gillian Rose, for example, has vividly described her own experiences moving about in public spaces as a woman and the heightened awareness that this gives her and other women of the relationship between space and power relations:

> I have a strong sense of space as oppressive, for example, from being scared walking at night in the city in which I live. I have to tell my own fears of attack in terms of space: when I've felt threatened, space suffocatingly surrounds me with an opacity that robs me of my right to be there; I cannot look around, the details surrounding me swamp me, the innocent transparency of the empty street becomes like an aggressive plastic lens pushing on me. Space almost becomes like an

enemy itself. This fear is partly about being defined as a woman.

(Rose 1993: 143)

This experience of space renders entry and movement about space hazardous, full of potential dangers. If relatively privileged women such as the middle-class, white academic Rose feel vulnerable, alienated or fearful when entering public spaces, highly aware of being watched and of their movements in space, women who are even more marginalized are subject to an even greater intensification of surveillance and the implicit threat of those who watch them. Sex workers, for example, disturb such boundaries as that distinguishing between private and public by inhabiting public spaces to invite strangers to perform acts with them that are deemed to be appropriate only in private relationships. Their presence on the streets is constantly challenged by police and other authorities, who attempt to 'clean up' the streets and make these spaces 'respectable' by removing them (Duncan 1996; Edelman 2011). In some cities, such as Washington, DC, special zones have been created within which sex workers are not allowed to solicit for clients or enter even if not seeking work. If individuals who are known to police as sex workers or are even suspected of engaging in sex work enter the 'Prostitution Free Zone', as it is called in Washington, DC, police offers are legally entitled to arrest them or order them to leave the zone (Edelman 2011).

So too, gay men and lesbians are constantly challenged in relation to their right to display their affection for members of the same sex in public, including such acts as kissing or holding hands which are unproblematic for heterosexuals.

Gay men and lesbians are subject to control by the legal and policing system as well as by heterosexuals, who may express their disapproval through stares, whispers or mutterings, or in more extreme ways with verbal abuse or physical violence. As a result, lesbians and gay men must constantly be on their guard in public places, policing their own behaviour and being wary of others' reactions and the imminent threat of open hostility and violence (Myslik 1996; Valentine 1996; Barron and Bradford 2007).

Strategies of spatial exclusion, therefore, are typically employed by members of dominant social groups to exert control over marginalized groups for which they hold hostility, contempt or fear of contamination. Such groups may be constructed as posing a risk to the dominant group through behaviour that is deemed to be too 'different' or potentially polluting and therefore confronting. The spaces these groups occupy are commonly singled out as dangerous and contaminating to the dominant groups. Alternatively, marginalized groups may be constructed as being vulnerable and 'at risk' from the greater power of the dominant group. For marginalized groups, constructed by dominant groups as the Other, requiring regulation or exclusion or both, this domination of space leads in turn to feelings of enhanced fear and anxiety, of being 'at risk' of intimidation, violence or coercion.

CONCLUDING COMMENTS

As this chapter has shown, ideas and strategies around risk often operate at the symbolic, conceptual level, organized around notions of Self and Other. Risk beliefs and practices, as they are employed in the deportment and experience of the body, therefore go beyond the need to exert control against the threat of particular hazards (pollution, toxins, terrorism, viruses or crime, for example). At the more symbolic level, the body is conceptualized as being 'at risk' when its autonomy and integrity appear to be threatened. Because the dominant ideal notion of the body is that of the body as controlled, its boundaries policed and regulated and kept separate from other bodies and the outside world, anything which appears to flout these boundaries, to break them down and allow intermingling of properly separate entities, is considered threatening, or 'risky'. Those bodies of others who are considered to lack the capacity for proper regulation of their bodily boundaries are routinely positioned as 'risky' to oneself. In Western societies, it is typically members of stigmatized or marginalized groups – women, the working class, the poor and unemployed, non-whites, injecting drug users, gays and lesbians – who are constructed as 'grotesque bodies' and therefore as 'risky' or 'at risk', needful of control, surveillance and discipline. It has also been argued, however, that constructions of Otherness also evoke feelings of fascination, excitement, desire, and that pleasure as well as anxiety is implicated in responses to the 'risky' Other. The next chapter takes up this question of risk and pleasure in greater detail.

8

RISK AND PLEASURE

Contemporary experts and popular cultures tend to represent risk as negative, something to be avoided. So too, much of the academic literature on risk represents individuals in late modernity as living in fear, constantly dogged by feelings of anxiety, vulnerability and uncertainty in relation to the risks of which they are constantly made aware. As observed in Chapter 1, risk is now often a synonym for danger or hazard, and the early modern concept of a 'good risk' appears largely to have been removed from the vernacular, appearing only in the parlance of economic speculation. As was argued in previous chapters, the emphasis in contemporary Western societies on the avoidance of risk is strongly associated with the ideal of the 'civilized' body, an increasing desire to take control over one's life, to rationalize and regulate the self and the body, to avoid the vicissitudes of fate. To take unnecessary risks is commonly seen as foolhardy, careless, irresponsible, and even 'deviant', evidence of an individual's ignorance or lack of ability to regulate the self.

Against these dominant discourses on risk, however, there also exists a counter-discourse, in which risk-taking is represented far more positively. Against the ideal of the highly controlled 'civilized' body/self is the discourse which valorizes escape from the bonds of control and regulation, expressing a hankering after the pleasures of the 'grotesque' body, the body that is more permeable and open to the world. This discourse rejects the ideal of the disembodied rational actor for an ideal of the self that emphasizes sensual embodiment and the visceral and emotional flights produced by encounters with danger, of 'walking on the wild side'. This chapter examines this counter-discourse on risk, beginning with a discussion of escape attempts and edgework, moving on to an analysis of the gendered nature of risk-taking as performative practices, and finishing with a discussion of desire and transgression.

ESCAPE ATTEMPTS

Since the late twentieth century there has been an expansion of participation in 'extreme sports' among people living in Western countries (Willig 2008). These sports include such activities as sky-diving, white-water rafting, swimming with sharks, big wave surfing, BASE jumping, abseiling, bungee-jumping, paragliding, rock-climbing, mountain-climbing and ice-climbing. They are called 'extreme sports' because they are seen to test the limits of human endurance for fear. Their central attraction is the courting of danger, the active taking of risks for the excitement and sense of achievement that they bring with them (Willig 2008; Brymer and Schweitzer 2012). Adventure holidays involving feats of extreme physical endurance and bravery have also become popular among some social groups. Expeditions to climb Mount Everest are now offered for people with minimal experience in mountain climbing. There is also a current trend for some travel companies to offer the traveller wanting a 'different' and challenging holiday the opportunity to engage in 'real-life' risky situations for a time, such as spending several days on the meanest streets of New York City, or accompanying an American bounty hunter on his mission to find and capture criminals. Further, a plethora of advertisements – particularly those that are oriented towards a youth market, selling such products as sporting goods, four-wheel drive cars, alcohol or soft drinks – have used images of risk-taking, often in rugged outdoors settings, to market their products, appealing to the target audience's desire to be 'different' and out of the ordinary in their willingness to face danger and seek out thrills.

The increasing presence of these cultural products suggests a growing fascination with the pleasures and excitement of risk-taking. Risk researchers have begun to focus on the affective dimensions of risk, understanding that the apprehension of a threat or catastrophe is often imbued with emotion, as is the desire to court risk as part of thrill-seeking or the need for excitement (Lupton and Tulloch 2002a). In their book, *Escape Attempts* (1976/1992), Cohen and Taylor discuss a number of ways in which individuals seek to transcend the banal, routine nature of everyday life, to 'escape and resist reality'. They argue that 'escape attempts' all involve some risks, from the minor risk of offending one's partner or friends, to major threatening of life and limb. Activities such as going on holiday or taking drugs are 'interruptions in the flow of life, interludes, temporary breaks, skirmishes, glimpses of other realities' (ibid.: 45). They are means of breaking the routine, albeit temporarily, and avoiding a sense of boredom and predictability and the dissatisfaction that may accompany them: 'We talk of routines as dull and dreary; phrases like "breaking out of the routine" suggest their oppressiveness, whilst a reference to something as "just routine" decreases the significance of the activity so described' (ibid.: 48).

Giddens (1990, 1991) has similarly observed that most people have an ambivalent emotional response to their established routines and habits. Routines, rituals and habits are important to the establishment and maintenance of ontological security, fostering a sense of familiarity, permanence and certainty. When routines are shattered, anxiety, fear and hostility may be produced (Giddens 1990: 98–9). However, people may also deliberately cultivate risks as a means of undermining ontological security:

> Such situations make possible the display of daring, resourcefulness, skill and sustained endeavour, where people are only too aware of the risks involved in what they are doing, but use them to create an edge which routine circumstances lack.
>
> (Giddens 1991: 132)

Activities engaged in for the sake of novelty often themselves become routine, and inevitably take place according to certain boundaries, norms and assumptions, or 'scripts' (Cohen and Taylor 1976/1992). It is perhaps only those activities that seem to counter taken-for-granted scripts, to transgress them in some way, that retain their excitement. Some risks, like the famous wild car trip taken by Hunter S. Thompson and his attorney while high on drugs between Los Angeles and Las Vegas, as recounted in his book *Fear and Loathing in Las Vegas* (1972), are part of adventures, requiring the active embracing of danger as part of the high: driving at high speeds while under the influence of various drugs, legal and illicit (Cohen and Taylor 1976/1992: 195–6).

> Excesses and outrages of all sorts must be built into the trip in order to transcend the limitations of ordinary landscaping, to construct a realm so far away from home that literally and metaphorically you are beyond reach … For such trips, you must take risks.
>
> (Cohen and Taylor 1976/1992: 196)

The discourse of release from the overly regulated body/self that appears in positive representations of risk-taking draws on a number of related discourses, including those that portray too tight a control over the self as a source of stress and illness and loss of self-authenticity. Participating in activities that are coded as dangerous or risky can bring an adrenalin rush that allows aficionados to escape the bounds of the rational mind and controlled body, to allow the body's sensations and emotions to overcome them for a time. There is a sense of heightened living, of being closer to nature than culture, of breaking the 'rules' that society is seen as imposing upon people (Lyng 1990, 2005; Willig 2008). At such times, participants in such activities may attempt to experience the sublimity of losing their selves in the moment, of transcending the constraints of 'civilized' behaviour.

This loss of self was championed by the Romantics in the eighteenth and early nineteenth centuries. For the Romantics, the turn towards emotion and feeling was important to avoid what they saw as the emotional sterility of modern life in its obsession with rational order and self-mastery.

Contemporary discourses of release often draw on neo-Romantic ideals, concerning the return to the authenticity of nature, the central role of emotion in self-expression (Lupton 1998: 81–2). One example is that of the German Green movement, in which 'to live is to survive, an opportunity to rediscover in more elementary, precarious, almost savage lifestyles, the sensations, pleasures, pains, difficulties, intoxication, and roughness of a life they imagine they lost with the advent of civilization' (Ewald 1993: 228). Similarly, in her study of 'New Age' Travellers, Wild (2005) notes that those who have chosen to identify as Travellers do so in part as an escape attempt, a desire for freedom from the norms of society and an opportunity to live a peripatetic life that is closer to nature and less confined by 'society'. Despite the stigmatized meanings of Otherness that adhere to Travellers, 'New Age' Travellers often actively choose their Otherness, structuring their identities via their marginalized status. Otherness, she argues, is part of a powerful affective dimension of the desire to be a 'New Age' Traveller, involving the choice to be outside the dominant social group, to transgress dominant expectations of behaviour and appearance. This decision produces a certain amount of existential uncertainty, but this uncertainty is embraced rather than shunned by these individuals.

The pleasures of risk-taking also inhere in the ways in which risk-takers may find a communal spirit with other like-minded souls. To engage in risky activities may bind people together closely in this common pursuit (Lyng 1990, 2005; Willig 2008). This may lead to a state of 'collective effervescence' (Mellor and Shilling 1997: 1), a Durkheimian term which refers to the intense emotionality produced through group activities. Durkheim used the term in relation to religious activities and spiritual elation. In the increasingly secular Western societies, collective effervescence is also produced in other communal activities, often those that seek heightened sensual embodied experiences. Examples include taking part in a riot, mass fight or war, being a member of a violent gang, engaging in dangerous physical activities with others or drinking to excess or taking drugs with others. Through the activities evoking communal effervescence, participants may lose a sense of their autonomous selves, becoming, at least for a brief time, part of a mass of bodies/selves with a common, shared purpose. This sense of losing one's boundaries, merging with others, may be experienced as frightening, but also as intensely pleasurable in the partial relinquishing of self-control and giving way to the collective will of the crowd (Maffesoli 1996; Mellor and Shilling 1997).

Voluntary risk-taking may also be viewed as a means of self-improvement, a form of working upon the self. This notion, which is commonly represented in self-help books, sees self-actualization in terms of a balance between opportunity and risk, choosing between an array of opportunities, some of which may be more 'risky' than others. From this perspective, risk-taking is viewed as a way of extending one's usual habits and activities out of a habituated 'comfort zone' and into a zone in which greater challenges are experienced. Giddens quotes a self-help book which argues that:

> If we reject deliberate risk-taking for self growth, we will inevitably remain trapped in our situation. Or we end up taking a risk unprepared. Either way, we have placed limits on our personal growth, have cut ourselves off from action in the service of high self-worth.
>
> (Giddens 1991: 78)

Some risks, therefore, are not to be avoided but rather embraced as part of the trajectory of self-actualization. To live a life that involves the avoidance of all risks, it is suggested in such literature, is to be stultified, moribund, and trapped in old habits and ways; to fail to develop as a person.

This concept of risk was identified in interviews with British people who engaged in extreme sports, which found that they saw their risk-taking as part of a 'wider aspirational project' to do with setting and meeting challenges and extending one's personal limitations (Willig 2008: 694). Doing so engendered feelings of satisfaction and accomplishment. The interviewees were aware that their feats of risk-taking also may provoke admiration and amazement from others at their courage and skills. They enjoyed recounting to others tales of their dare-doing and impressing them. Their activities made these interviewees feel different from the majority of people who lacked this willingness to engage in extreme sports and gave them a sense of pride in their own abilities to stand out from the crowd in such a way (ibid.).

Similarly, in research John Tulloch and I undertook involving interviews with Australians about their concepts of risk, a common discourse centred on the importance of voluntary risk-taking as contributing to one's life project. As one interviewee noted, 'life would be pretty dull without risk' (Lupton and Tulloch 2002a: 117). The interviewees discussed how risk-taking was a means of giving momentum to their lives, saving them from stasis and boredom. According to this discourse, voluntary risk-taking impels movement and progression. It may not simply involve physical risk-taking, such as participation in extreme sports, but can also include taking creative risks as an artist or performer, travelling or moving to a different country, 'coming out' as gay or resisting gender stereotypes. Our interviewees also discussed the camaraderie of risk-taking, feeling part of a group, the emotional intensities they experienced when choosing to take risks and the pleasure they experienced from taking risks and yet feeling in control.

Some people also choose to engage in activities that are culturally coded as 'risky' because of a deliberate attempt to resist cultural norms, to exhibit willingness to transgress assumptions of behaviour, or because the pleasures associated with the risks are valued more highly than the apparent dangers. People may accept expert knowledge on risk as valid but yet proceed with engaging in a behaviour deemed 'risky' despite this acceptance because of what they perceive to be the benefits of engaging in the behaviour. This is particularly evident in research on illicit drug taking. Such research describes the pleasures that people experience when taking drugs such as Ecstasy, cocaine or heroin or when inhaling substances such as glue or aerosol paints. The pleasures involved are not only the embodied effects of the drug, but also the notion that one is conforming to a desired sub-culture, or resisting authority. Engaging in such officially proscribed activities as using drugs may be part of experimentation about 'what the body can do', pressing up against limits imposed by expert or authoritative knowledges (Fox 2002). People may also engage in illicit drug use because of a desire to overcome feelings of anxiety, depression or pain caused by abusive, traumatic, marginalized or disadvantaged life experiences (Valentine and Fraser 2008).

The sheer embodied pleasures produced by illicit or legal drugs (such as alcohol and cigarettes) are also important to acknowledge (Valentine and Fraser 2008; Bunton and Coveney 2011; Dennis 2011). Drug users report how much they enjoy the 'rush' that drugs give them, the physical sensations that overwhelm their bodies and allow them to escape their thoughts and worries for a time. Although the biochemical processes of addiction may also be involved, the sheer pleasures of using are such that many drug users seek out their drug simply for these moments of embodied sensation (MacLean 2008; Valentine and Fraser 2008). Even the realization that such drugs may damage one's body or even lead to death may contribute to the intensity of the pleasure of using them (MacLean 2008). Similarly, taking physical risks during such activities as extreme sports is a way of testing the capabilities of one's body, seeking to overcome fear and panic. Once the danger has passed and been dealt with successfully, participants often experience intense feelings of well-being and exhilaration (Brymer and Schweitzer 2012; see also the discussion of edgework below).

The concept of addiction and its emotional intensities has been brought together with that of assemblages to theorize young men's compulsion towards violence in war zones and other condoned spaces of violence such as city drinking spots (Jayne *et al.* 2010; Aitken 2012). It has been argued that addictive assemblages of violence are configured in such spaces to the point that the men involved in violent acts experience a craving to constantly engage in them again and again. The hard bodies and hard emotions that are produced via the strategies and spaces of military training conform to a hegemonic masculinity in which violence becomes part of male bonding and masculine identity. In such analyses the spaces and material objects, as well as the other bodies with which people interact contribute to this assemblage. Long periods of boredom, often in confined spaces, waiting for something to happen, the presence and ready availability of weapons and interaction with other combatants, in combination with training strategies and dominant discourses privileging violence and the sheer emotional intensity of the fight, are all integral to the addictive assemblage of violence (Aitken 2012). So too, in the context of the city, alcohol, concepts of hegemonic masculinities, race and youth and encounters with others' bodies combine with the spatial dimensions in which drinking occurs to produce specific addictive assemblages of violence (Jayne *et al.* 2010).

EDGEWORK

The concept of 'edgework' was first developed by Stephen Lyng (1990, 2005, 2008; Lyng and Matthews 2007). Lyng (1990) took the term 'edgework' from Hunter S. Thompson's writings, and used it to apply to participants' experiences in dangerous activities that are undertaken as part of leisure pursuits. The concept has since been extended to include such diverse activities as involvement in a search-and-rescue team

(Lois 2005), self-starvation (Gailey 2009), sadomasochistic sexual practices (Newmahr 2011), market-trading on the stock exchange (Smith 2005), and young women's criminal activity (Bachelor 2007).

Edgework incorporates the notion that risk-taking activities are about exploring the edges that exist along boundaries, a form of boundary negotiation. These boundaries may include those between sanity and insanity, consciousness and unconsciousness, life and death and an ordered sense of self and environment against a disordered sense of self and environment. (Lyng 2005: 4). Edgework involves the following dimensions of risk-taking: it is voluntary; it is undertaken for a specific purpose; it involves skill to negotiate danger and avoid serious injury or death; and it is undertaken as part of a desire to experience intense emotion, vitality, hyper-reality and being 'in the moment' and to temporarily escape the demands and alienation of the mundane everyday world. Edgework is undertaken as part of the project of the self in the effort to achieve self-actualization, a more 'real' self. Edgework is also characterized by an emphasis on skilled performance of the dangerous activity, involving the ability to maintain control over a situation that verges on complete chaos that requires, above all, 'mental toughness' and the ability not to give in to fear (Lyng 1990: 859).

Edgeworkers commonly describe a sense of blurring of the boundaries between themselves and the technologies under their control (kayaks, climbing ropes, parachutes, racing cars, motor cycles, and so on), so that they have a sense of 'being one with their machines'. When talking about edgework, they note that what they deem important is not to override fear but to acknowledge its presence and convert it into something that is sensually appealing. This involves an acceptance of fear combined with confidence that one can act skilfully to avoid accident or death. Edgework therefore does not involve the complete relinquishment of control: to do so would be tantamount to attempting suicide or self-harming. So too, the emotional dimensions of voluntary risk-taking are more complex than simply involving the desire to incite intense emotions. It may not only be the feelings involved that are valued, but the individual's ability to master and control these emotions. When they are able to exert mastery over emotions that are viewed as negative, people experience heightened feelings of control (Lyng 1990, 2005, 2008; Smith 2005; Brymer and Schweitzer 2012).

For example, when participating in white-water kayaking, it is important to maintain control over fear so that the kayak will stay afloat and will be able to navigate the hazards of the water it is traversing. It is the individual's awareness of maintaining this control, despite experiencing intense sensations of fear and excitement, which produces a sense of elation. Market traders similarly experience a rush from keeping their heads within a turbulent, chaotic environment (Smith 2005). This combination of intense emotional arousal and focused attention leads to edgeworkers experiencing alterations in perception of time and space, feelings of hyper-reality which lead to a sense of the experience as deeply authentic, as feeling truly alive (Lyng and Matthews, 2007).

Those who engage in edgework often express the belief that 'mental toughness' is an innate ability, possessed by only a select and elite few. To take risks, therefore, is considered by such individuals not as foolhardy but rather as evidence of superior qualities that allow people to court danger without harming themselves (Lyng 1990). This attitude is often articulated by such well-known wealthy adventurers as English entrepreneur Richard Branson who attempt perilous and highly-publicized feats such as circling the globe in a hot-air balloon as an alternative route of excitement and achievement. It is also evident in the words of a 16-year-old Australian boy discussing the pleasure of 'train-surfing', or riding a moving train on its roof:

> It's so much fun. When you get off the train you feel like a superior being sometimes. You know some call it stupid, but you just love it. It's stupid in other people's eyes but they just don't understand and you don't expect them to.
>
> (quoted in *The Age* newspaper, 6 October 1997)

As noted above, there is another meaning that is associated with voluntary risk-taking: that which represents it as part of the reflexive project of the self in terms of achieving personal 'growth'. From this perspective risk-taking is considered vital to self-realization and improvement. Lyng (1990: 860) found that among the parachute jumpers to whom he spoke, the notions of 'self-realization', 'self-actualization' and 'self-determination' were commonly claimed as goals of engaging in their dangerous activity: 'In the pure form of edgework, individuals experience themselves as instinctively acting entities, which leaves them with a purified and magnified sense of self' (ibid.: 860). Cultivated risk-taking in this context is seen to provide an opportunity for individuals to display courage, to master fear, to prove something to themselves which allows them to live life with a sense of personal agency: 'Having survived the challenge, one feels capable of dealing with any threatening situation' (ibid.: 860).

In discourses that privilege risk-taking there is therefore some reliance upon this quest for self-authenticity. Taking risks is sometimes seen as relinquishing the control of one's behaviour imposed by society, stepping outside and resisting expectations, being spontaneous, seizing the day. The risk-taker may be viewed as someone who possesses courage, not only in placing her or himself in danger but also in her or his deliberate contravening of societal norms. There is something extraordinary about the risk-taker. The person who attempts to sail or hot-air balloon around the world single-handed, the mountain climber scaling a dangerous peak, the daring entrepreneur who makes millions in business through taking risks, are all seen to stand out from the pack. Such risk-takers are often admired for their courage and strength of will and purpose, their willingness to face danger, to gamble with uncertainty.

Much of the edgework literature focuses on individuals and their experiences rather than examining it as a shared, interdependent or collaborative experience in which people must rely on others in their navigation of the edge. Such collaborative edgework incorporates others both constructing the boundaries of the edge as well as helping to transgress it safely. One example is that of sadomasochistic (SM) activities, in which those who participate must finely judge how much pain to seek or inflict, reading from their own and others' emotions and physical responses when developing these assessments (Newmahr 2011). The boundaries in SM are emotional and psychological as well as physical and always collaboratively negotiated and constituted. They are impossible to transgress alone: they always require at least one other participant. For SM participants, the edges they challenge or transgress are those between liberty and constraint, kindness and cruelty, control and loss of control, comfort and punishment, and goodness and badness. They must invest their trust in the other participants that they will not make a poor judgement that will result in serious physical injury or death, to remain rational despite experiencing intense emotions such as anger, fear, humiliation, the urge to hurt or physically restrain someone or to be hurt or restrained (ibid.).

Edgework can represent both a challenge to limits, everyday routines and social expectations, but paradoxically, also as an expression of dominant institutional demands and imperatives: to be entrepreneurial in the business world, for example, by voluntarily taking risks as part of the attempt to increase productivity and profits (Lyng 2005; Smith 2005). While these two sides of edgework may seem to be contradictory, they may also be viewed as complementary. The skills and expertise derived from leisure-based risk-taking practices may be employed to win success in the workplace, for example (Lyng 2005: 10). A positive approach to risk-taking currently dominates in the sites of work and employment, particularly in relation to high-level managerial positions or those areas in which people are expected to demonstrate 'creativity', such as in marketing and advertising. Contests encouraging people to pit themselves against each other and to compete in terms of demonstrating daring are common in most institutionalized risk environments, including the economic sector (Giddens 1991: 132). The contemporary vogue for exhaustive testing of aspirants to positions using a battery of psychological and other tests often include probing them for their responses to potentially risky situations. Questionnaires ask people, for example, whether they would like to go scuba diving, or whether they ever fantasized about being a race car driver. Those who answer such questions in the affirmative are marked out as being willing to step out of conventional patterns of behaviour, to seek alternative ways of doing things – that is, to take risks. This is valued in a professional workplace where 'flexibility' is a buzz word (Martin 1994).

In experiential training methods popular in the United States and elsewhere, workers are encouraged to engage in physical activities designed to test their will-power and fortitude and to develop a sense of 'survival' and responsiveness to the rapidly changing business environment, including taking risks, tolerating fear and being innovative (Martin 1994). The experiences are designed to arouse fear and excitement to serve as models for workers' experiences in unpredictable work situations. They may include such activities as climbing and leaping off high towers and telegraph poles, walking across a high wire and abseiling down cliffs. The idea is that 'rigidity' is avoided for 'flexibility' and the ability to 'adapt' to changing conditions. Taking risks is viewed as one means of adapting to a changing environment. Risk-taking, therefore, in the work context may be considered part of an overall strategy for career advancement. The notion is that once a person has reached a certain level in their career, they may need to take a risk – to move to another position, perhaps involving a cut in salary – in order to achieve long-term goals. Risk-taking becomes the mark of someone who is ambitious and not content with remaining at a plateau in their career. The importance of personal flexibility is again implicated in this notion of risk-taking.

Thus there may be said to be a degree of synergy between the skills, competencies and symbolic resources engendered via participation in edgework practices and the demands of late modernity. Linking in with the risk society thesis, this approach to edgework sees it as integral to risk society. If risks and uncertainties are viewed as pervasive throughout the domains of social life, and confronting and managing risk are viewed as part of the late modern subject position, then edgework may also be seen as part of everyone's everyday lives. This edgework is not engaged in because of desire to escape everyday life: it is an integral dimension of everyday life. Edgework is simultaneously part of efforts to transcend institutional imperatives in some contexts (dangerous leisure activities, for example) and in others a vital dimensions of conforming to these imperatives.

Risk-taking may be regarded as the flipside of modernity, a response to the ever-intensifying focus on control and predictability of modernity. On the other hand, however, the preparedness to take risks converges with some of the most basic orientations of modernity: 'The capability to disturb the fixity of things, open up new pathways, and thereby colonise a segment of a novel future, is integral to modernity's unsettling character' (Giddens 1991: 133). The current insistent presence of risk may be associated with new modes of conduct and self-formation, the invention of new experiences of life and pleasures in response to the social changes emerging in late modernity (Ewald 1993). The contemporary subject may be understood to require both routine and risk: to hanker after both predictability and unpredictability, constantly oscillating between the two. An excess of one state leads to a fervent desire for the other. Heightened awareness of risk may itself lead to a desire to take risk. Indeed, predict-ability itself may be viewed as a risk. Cohen and Taylor quote a slogan which argues, 'We do not want a world in which the guarantee of no longer dying of hunger is exchanged for the risk of dying of boredom' (1976/1992: 160).

RISK-TAKING AS GENDERED PERFORMANCES

Of all social groups, it is probably young people, and par-ticularly young men, who most often take risks as part of their everyday lives. Drinking to excess and taking other drugs, speeding in cars, engaging in petty theft and train-surfing are ways of adding thrills to life, testing one's bound-aries of fear and endurance, proving one's adulthood or masculinity. Such activities are attempts to engage in the 'heroic life', which involves deeds of virtuosity, courage, adventure, endurance and the capacity to attain distinction and a higher purpose through the risking of life itself (Featherstone 1995: 55). This higher purpose need not be altruistic, as in the archetype of the hero, but may also be a desire to achieve heights of sublimity. Transcending every-day life becomes an end and purpose in itself. Importantly, the discourse of the heroic life as it is counterpoised against everyday life is profoundly gendered: 'A basic contrast, then, is that the heroic life is the sphere of danger, violence and the courting of risk whereas the everyday life is the sphere of women, reproduction and care' (ibid.: 59).

Other analyses have identified young men as a sub-cultural group most likely to engage in activities that are deemed 'risky' as a means of performing dominant mascu-linities. Collison (1996) has discussed how young English working-class men in a young offenders prison described engaging in predatory street crime activities and taking drugs for the thrill of 'living on the edge'. He notes that for these young men, '[e]dgework represents a sometimes spontaneous search for a dramatic self within a world of alienation and over-socialization ... Being on the edge, or over it – beyond reason and in passion – is momentarily to grasp a spiritual and romantic Utopia' (ibid.: 435). As these comments suggest, in a sociocultural context in which dominant forms of masculinity privilege the ability to keep one's body/self separate from others, to be self-contained and autonomous, to be hard and dry, the opportunity to engage in risk-taking achieves several ends. Not only does such risk-taking demonstrate courage and sometimes the enhanced capacity for self-control and bodily containment, it may also allow men to relax the tight control that is expected of them, if only for a short time and in limited ways. To engage in dangerous activities, for example, may demonstrate a man's control over the emotions of fear, vulnerability and anxiety, proving to others and himself the expanded limits of his control of self and the body. At the same time it affords him the opportunity to experience and enjoy heightened emotion and exhilaration.

Some other occasions of risk-taking, however, may involve letting loose emotions in ways that are seen to bolster masculinity: as in fighting, for example, or drinking to excess. Such activities allow men to test and define their boundaries of selfhood and embodiment through occasional excess. As noted above, the concept of assemblages has been used to describe the ways in which normative concepts of masculinity, men's own bodies, those of other people, the spaces and places in which they are sited and the material objects to which they have access (weapons, alcohol and other drugs, cars and so on) come together to configure specific addictive or risk-taking assemblages.

The popular media frequently draw upon and reproduce gendered notions of risk-taking in representing heroic figures. The figure of the round-the-world sailor, the mountain climber, is predominantly masculine, engaging in masculine-coded feats. The rare woman who engages in such activities is portrayed as though she were unique in her desire and ability to emulate these feats. Such a woman's achievement is seen as even more unusual because of her gender. The heroic male figure of action films throws himself into danger without a moment's thought, actively seeking situations in which he risks his life and both receives and deals out brutal violence. While there are some equally courageous and fool-hardy female characters in mainstream film and television series (such as the Ripley character played by Sigourney Weaver in the *Alien* series and the women in the *Charlie's Angels* television series and feature film), they remain few in number compared with the male heroes. Female characters, in the main, continue to serve as the passive onlookers on masculine heroic risk-taking, often positioned as the reason why men must place themselves in danger, so as to rescue their women or return home to them.

While men may engage in risk-taking in the attempt to conform to dominant forms of masculinity, women's concepts of risk-taking are also highly related to assumptions about femininity. Risk-taking is less valorized for the performance of femininity: indeed, dominant notions of femininity tend to represent the careful avoidance of danger and hazard as important. Women are acculturated from an early age to avoid situations of danger and are represented as particularly vulnerable to such risks as sexual assault and mugging because of their gender. They are more often portrayed as the passive victims of risk than as active risk-takers. As I noted in Chapter 7, women's bodies are culturally represented as more prone to chaos and disorder compared with men's bodies. Control over the self may therefore be even more sought after by women than by men. In this context, women who find the constraints imposed by cultural notions of femininity may seek to counter these by deliberating engaging in masculine-coded risk-taking activities or other activities that allow them to 'let go' to some extent of the control that is expected of them. While the dominant masculine notion of risk-taking may revolve around placing oneself in situations courting injury or death, many women see risk-taking as related to expressing their sexuality.

For example, in her essay on the pleasures of dancing in nightclubs as a woman, Gotfrit (1991) describes the physical delight, sensualities and eroticism of dancing to loud dance music in the public realm of the nightclub dance floor. She notes that the dance floor is 'a rare public place where letting go of the tight rein women often keep on their sexuality is possible, where the pleasures of the body are embraced and privileged' (ibid.: 178–9). Accompanied by the sensual pleasures of dancing is the contextualization of the night-club as a sexually-charged place of 'unknown possibilities', where dancing might be seen as a preamble to flirting, romance and sex. In this account, therefore, central to the diffuse pleasures and sensualities of dancing are the notions of risk and danger implicated with losing control, being swept away, taking a leap into the unknown by engaging erotically with a stranger. Gotfrit goes on to describe the feeling of 'naughtiness' or

> [a] benign sense of mischief involved in the dancing experience, of doing things that she otherwise would avoid, such as daring to be potentially 'bad' by staying up late, participating in a sleazy nightclub, wearing short skirts and allowing herself to feel desire and be desired, of 'stepping out of "good girl" territory'.
>
> (Gotfrit 1991: 180)

She conceptualizes her pleasure as being associated with resistance, particularly to dominant notions of appropriate femininity as asexual and contained in space. In dancing in a nightclub, women are able to privilege their bodies, to experience desire and sensual pleasure and express their sexuality, to boldly take up space and to allow their pleasure in dancing to overcome their self-consciousness about the need to exert rigid control over their feminine embodiment.

Edgework research has predominantly focused on male risk-takers, the vast majority of whom are white and middle-class. These men are able to afford to engage in such activities as 'adventure holidays' or extreme sporting pursuits. Women and men who are from marginalized and disempowered social groups may experience edgework differently. A study of young Scottish women imprisoned for engaging in violent behaviour and other criminal activities such as stealing and illicit drug use (Bachelor 2007) found that these women were initially drawn to engage in this behaviour because of the shared adrenaline 'rush' or 'buzz' they felt, a desire to escape boredom and to feel as if they could foster friendships and belonged to a group. Some of these young women participated in these activities because of an attraction towards traditional masculinities and the feeling of power and toughness this afforded them. However, they increasingly came to undertake such activities as a means of blocking out powerful emotions such as grief and rage caused by life experiences of abuse, family dysfunction and institutional care. These young women remarked that they often felt 'emotionally numb' and 'detached' and that risk-taking was a way of making them feel more alive. For these women, violent behaviour, self-harm and drug use were ways of feeling different, either by blocking out conscious thoughts which were distressing, evoking feelings of power and control when feeling powerless and helpless or venting feelings of anger and hurt by hurting others. They were not taking risks to escape the alienating world of work and to achieve a sense of authenticity and hyper-reality, as do privileged white men. Instead, they were attempting to achieve a sense of control over a world in which they felt increasingly disempowered. They were also seeking a way of feeling close to others (their peer-group) in a context in which their families had not provided intimacy and caring and a sense of belonging.

Interviews with American mountain search-and-rescue volunteers found a gendered difference in the ways in which the male and female team-members described the emotional management involved in this activity (Lois 2005). These volunteers were called upon to remain calm in highly physically dangerous and emotionally challenging situations, involving helping injured people, rescuing people from avalanche-prone terrain, rafters from rapids, and rock-climbers from cliff faces or retrieving dead bodies from accidents or plane crashes. They were required to deal with their own and others' fear, anxiety, panic, distress and disgust, as well as guilt and sadness if they felt they had been unable to help someone. Like edgeworkers engaging in leisure pursuits such as sky-diving and rock-climbing, these volunteers enjoyed the opportunity to exert control over their feelings and physical reactions to danger and gruesome sights such as mutilated bodies or finding someone dead whom they knew. Unlike those who engage in leisure-based edgework, however, the volunteers were sometimes confronted with the requirement to manage distressing emotions in response to the human suffering they constantly encountered so as to re-establish a sense of control and continue in their edgework activities.

This study found that male rescuers were similar to Lyng's sky-divers in terms of expressing confidence that they were able to control their emotions in the dangerous situations in which they found themselves and describing an innate ability to do this successfully. However, the female rescuers expressed greater feelings of trepidation about how they would cope and commented that they found it more difficult than the men to control their emotions during rescue work. These differing responses may be due to dominant cultural expectations about how women and men deal with and discuss intense emotions. It may have been difficult for the male rescuers to acknowledge to another person that they sometimes struggled to manage their emotions. Similarly, the female rescuers may have felt reluctant to position themselves as unemotional, as this may imply a lack of caring, a strongly feminized attribute.

Other women conceptualize risk-taking as challenging archetypes of feminine passivity by engaging in activities that are strongly coded as masculine. Olstead (2011) argues that women who engage in edgework may do so as political activity to resist or counter the gendered meanings attributed to risk and fear. In her interviews with four Canadian women who engaged in typically male edgework (sky-diving, rock-climbing and forest fire management), she found that the women tended to represent themselves as emotionally controlled, disengaged and highly regulated in the context of their urban environs. By contrast, in the context of the rural settings in which they participated in edgework, the women recounted experiences of feeling wild and emotionally engaged, closer to nature and their 'real selves'. The women noted that they were constantly urged by others to be 'responsible' and 'safe' and to avoid taking physical risks as much as possible and thus to conform to the norms of socially sanctioned risk-avoidant and responsible femininity. The women sought to subvert these norms by emphasizing their autonomy and independence in risk-taking, their capacity to deal with and control fear.

As this suggests, the dynamic and variegated nature of femininities and masculinities have implications for the gendered meanings of risk-taking. While risk-taking has been most closely linked to the performance of dominant masculinities, and risk avoidance is associated with dominant femininities, there is evidence of some shifts in these meanings. Dominant notions linking certain risk-taking activities with masculinity have begun to be challenged by some women, who have sought to perform alternative femininities through engaging in such activities.

DESIRE AND TRANSGRESSION

We referred in Chapter 7 to the ambivalence provoked by Otherness, the mixture of fear, disgust and anxiety and fascination and desire that Otherness tends to inspire. At the symbolic or psychodynamic level of meaning, it may be argued that the pleasures and exhilaration associated with risk-taking may emerge from the transgression of such conceptual boundaries (Sibley 1995: 32). While we may constantly seek to maintain conceptual boundaries, our very efforts impart a special power and significance to that which is defined as transgressive.

Sexual intercourse, for example, derives much of its excitement and pleasure for many because of its status as 'dirty' and 'forbidden', the transgressions of bodily boundaries it involves, the intermingling of usually reviled bodily fluids: 'Sex is perceived as dirty, bestial, smelly, messy, sticky, slimy, oozy, and that is precisely, for many, its attraction' (Miller 1997: 127). Cohen and Taylor (1976/1992: 129) argue that some forms of sexuality – particularly those that are culturally represented as 'deviant', such as homosexuality or sadomasochism, or socially prohibited, such as adultery – are particularly exciting because of their association with guilt, fear or anxiety: 'the "specialness" of the experience, and therefore its potential escape status is oddly enough related to the degree to which it is accompanied by fear, guilt and anxiety' (ibid.: 129). They contend that the more such sexual activity is 'liberated' and thereby rendered more mainstream and less 'deviant', the more banal it will be become, losing its status as an extreme escape attempt.

In the final chapter of *Purity and Danger* (1966/1969) Douglas comments on the paradoxical nature of our yearning for the pure and our repudiation of the unclean. Purity is 'the enemy of change, of ambiguity and compromise' (ibid.: 162). When accomplished, purity is 'poor' and 'barren'; it is 'hard and dead as a stone when we get it' (ibid.: 161). Notions of purity are also beset with contradictions, or enforce hypocrisy. For example, ideas of sexual purity, if taken to their extreme, deny all sexual contact between the sexes, leading to the extinction of a culture (ibid.: 162). Cultures deal with this by rendering that which is defiling to be most sacred, allowing contact with it at certain prescribed times and places. By its very nature of lying outside, of being forbidden, that which is categorized as 'dirt', as 'polluting' is powerful:

> The danger which is risked by boundary transgression is power. Those vulnerable margins and those attacking forces which threaten to destroy good order represent the powers inhering in the cosmos. Ritual which can harness these for good is harnessing power indeed.
>
> (Douglas 1966/1969: 161)

Indeed, religions often render sacred those things that are defined as impure. By this process the impure retains its special power, but becomes not destructive but creative. Some unclean things, but not all, are used constructively in ritual: blood in Jewish and Christian traditions, for example, is sacralized (Douglas 1966/1969: 159).

More secular rituals may also seek to overturn the negative meanings associated with the 'impure' by revelling in its very prohibited nature at certain prescribed times and places. Analyses of the medieval and early modern carnival as a popular cultural form in Europe have demonstrated the use of the carnivalesque as a means of transgressing binary oppositions, particularly that between high and low (Bakhtin 1984; Stallybrass and White 1986; Burke 1994). The carnivalesque body provided a way of disrupting boundaries, of calling into question accepted norms of bodily deportment and thereby disturbing the social order. Carnivalesque activities included ritual spectacles such as fairs and shows, games, popular feasts and wakes, processions and competitions, comic shows, circuses, mummery and dancing, open-air entertainment, the use of costumes and masks, parodies, farce, jokes, puns and tricks, curses and slang and other forms of folk humour (Stallybrass and White 1986: 8).

In the carnival season in early modern Europe, which began in late December or January and reached its apotheosis after Lent, feasting and excessive drinking were central to the activities. Carnival, the festivities of 'the world turned upside down', had three major themes, both real and symbolic: food, sex and violence (Burke 1994: 186). Meat consumption had particular significance as liberation from the austerities of Lent (indeed the name 'carnival' springs from the Latin word for meat). Rituals celebrated sexuality, and weddings often took place during carnival festivities. Aggressive and violent acts were depicted symbolically in rituals, but real acts of violence also took place, such as fighting among revellers, the torturing or killing of domestic animals or the stoning of Jews, and carnival was accepted as the time in which one could insult one's fellows freely. Inversions and transgressions were pivotal activities of carnival.

Dressing in costume was also central to carnival festivities, including men dressing as women, women as men and lay people in the costumes of clerics. It was common for people to costume themselves as devils, fools, wild men and wild animals. Popular prints of carnival depicted reversals of the relationship between humans and animals, such as the ox turned butcher, carving up a man, or of hierarchical relationships between humans, such as the son beating his father, servants giving orders to their masters, the poor giving alms to the rich, the husband holding the baby and spinning while the wife smokes and holds a gun (Burke 1994: Chapter 7).

The rituals and celebrations of carnival, therefore, served to challenge traditional hierarchies, at least for a time, allowing temporary liberation from routine constraints, controls and the established order. The carnivalesque was about ritualistic inversion, excess and hybridity: it was fundamentally about corporeality rather than disembodied rationality. Unlike 'high' cultural forms, the carnival celebrated the lower strata, including that of the human body. The vulgar, 'grotesque' body was privileged over the bourgeois, civilized body (Bakhtin 1984; Stallybrass and White 1986: Introduction). The openings and orifices of the body, and the fluids they ingested or emitted, were emphasized, and the lower regions of the body given priority over its upper regions (Stallybrass and White 1986: 9). The 'grotesque' carnival body either served to directly oppose the 'low' with the 'high' or else was formed through a process of hybridization or intermixing of binary opposites and elements usually thought of as incompatible (ibid.: 44). These transgressions inspired not fear, anxiety or repulsion, but rather pleasure, excitement, exhilaration, desire.

However, there were limits to behaviours in carnival. It was not simply a case of allowing anarchic behaviour to flourish. The rituals and traditions of the carnivalesque served to maintain certain boundaries and abuse weaker as well as stronger social groups such as women and ethnic and religious minorities. It therefore did not do away with the dominant culture and the official hierarchy, challenging them only temporarily. Some carnivalesque activities, for example, served to scapegoat and pillory outsiders and punish unruly women by humiliating them (Stallybrass and White 1986: 24). Stallybrass and White use the term 'displaced abjection' to refer to the process by which '"low" social groups turn their figurative and actual power, *not* against those in authority, but against those who are even "lower" (women, Jews, animals, particularly cats and pigs)' (ibid.: 53, original emphasis). Nonetheless, carnival activities have also been historically associated with political resistance and were not only about hedonistic revelry – revolts and rebellions often took place at times of major festivals (Burke 1994: 203–4).

While many activities associated with the pre-modern carnivalesque may have disappeared by the eighteenth century, there remain elements of the carnivalesque in modern and late-modern culture. The disavowal of carnival by the eighteenth-century bourgeois meant that it became the festival of the Other. While the bourgeoisie into the nineteenth and twentieth centuries denied the transgressive elements, the 'grotesque' body of the carnival, they also defined themselves through this suppression. Their participation in carnival became voyeuristic, partial, guilty and ambivalent. The fair or carnival, for example, was gradually marginalized and confined to certain areas, banished from wealthy areas.

In England, the outdoor carnivalesque site of pleasure moved to the seaside resort (Stallybrass and White 1986; Burke 1994: Chapter 9).

In the early twenty-first century, such sites as the resort, the fun fair, the music festival and theme and amusement parks provide the opportunity to engage in modern versions of the carnivalesque. Such activities as Mardi Gras parades (such as those that occur annually in Rio de Janeiro and Sydney) and agricultural shows or fairs are some of the few examples of pre-modern-style mass carnivalesque events that still occur in Western societies. However, these activities tend to be under the tight control of dominant social groups. Carnivalesque activities in contemporary Britain involving minority groups such as blacks and Gypsies are heavily policed and contained (Sibley 1995: 44–5). The subordination of marginalized groups, therefore, is often confirmed through their participation in and association with the carnivalesque.

The marginalized and despised, those social groups which are considered threatening and polluting, are often the subject of fascination and desire because of their very difference, their Otherness. Rejection and repudiation of the Other, therefore, are not simply about exclusion, but also involve the inclusion of the Other into self-identity. The attempt to expel and contain the Other is inevitably implicated with the production of desire and the emotions of nostalgia, longing and fascination (Stallybrass and White 1986: 191). As a consequence, the bourgeoisie is

> perpetually rediscovering the carnivalesque as a radical source of transcendence. Indeed that act of rediscovery itself, in which the middle classes excitedly discover their

own pleasures and desires under the sign of the Other, in
the realm of the Other, is constitutive of the very formation
of middle-class identity.

(Stallybrass and White 1986: 201)

As noted in Chapter 7, the black body, for example, has
been dominantly represented in white cultures as both sexually revolting and intensely erotically attractive. A significant feature of both responses to black bodies is their
cultural coding as different from white bodies, particularly
as more animalistic, more sexual, more primitive and closer
to nature. Sexual encounters of white bodies with non-
white bodies have typically attracted the meanings of forbidden desire and transgressive pleasures. Non-white
bodies, both male and female, have been represented in
white discourses as simultaneously inferior because of their
imputed 'uncivilized' animality, and superior for the same
reason: their 'animal' potency and allure. They have been
portrayed as both potentially defiling and as intensely erotically attractive in their very exotic nature, their cultural
position as Other. This would suggest that the boundary
between disgust and desire is very tenuous. Nineteenth-
century writings by the British on other races, particularly
Africans, while replete with expressions of repulsion, were
also often characterized by references to their beauty,
attractiveness or desirability (Young 1995). One writer,
Thomas Hope, described in an essay published in 1831 some
of the black 'varieties of human races' as 'disgusting', 'repul-
sive' and 'hideously ugly'. However, he also noted of members of 'certain Nubian nations' that: 'Their complexion
indeed still is dark, but it is the glossy black of marble or of

jet, conveying to the touch sensations more voluptuous even than those of the most resplendent white' (quoted in ibid.: 97).

An interesting analysis of contemporary luxury ice cream advertisements using naked black models to sell the product showed that the forbidden and transgressive eroticism of the black body was used to convey these meanings to the ice cream, and vice versa (Nakak 1997). Thus, for example, an advertisement for 'Deep Chocolate' flavour showed an image of a white man diving from a springboard into chocolate-flavoured ice-cream, shaped in curves to look like black breasts or buttocks. The copy suggested that eating this ice-cream was akin to the overwhelming and wicked pleasures of engaging in sexual activity with black bodies: 'If intensity scares you, great pleasure upsets you or love makes you flee, please don't try our new Deep Chocolate Ice Creams. The shock of real Callebaut Belgium chocolate might be a tad overwhelming… Surrender or stay away' (quoted in ibid.: 66–7). This imagery and text imply titillation that is similar to the ways in which pornography is advertised. It supports the notion that interracial sexual relations is a specialist, transgressive pleasure for whites that is suffused with particular intensity and thrills (ibid.).

Another example of the pleasure and desire produced by transgression is the contemporary horror film, which, like its predecessor the Gothic genre of literature, is preoccupied with transgression of cultural boundaries, with excess over order and fantasy, desire, sado-masochistic eroticism and strongly felt emotion over everyday realities. The Gothic novel was preoccupied with supernatural horror, with scenes of the torturing of a young female victim in the claustrophobic space of deserted and decayed castles, typically combined with romance and eroticism (Schubart 1995: 225). Both the horror film and the Gothic novel reveal traces of the repressed, those thoughts and feelings that are pushed into the unconscious because of their transgressive nature. In their focus on the figure of the monster, which commonly blurs boundaries between the living and the dead, the human and the supernatural, the human and animal, the human and machine, male and female, solid and liquid, the horror film and Gothic novel allow the projection of repressed and disturbing emotions such as desire, hatred, fear and disgust upon this Other. Ambivalent emotions are therefore central to the horror film experience, incorporating both fascination and pleasure with fear and dread (Schubart 1995; Tudor 1995). This genre remains popular in the contemporary era, with the *Twilight* book and film series drawing upon aspects of it in their focus on romantic longing, repressed desires, the erotic appeal of the Other and the breaching of bodily boundaries engendered by vampirism.

In summary, then, transgression is a potent source of pleasure as well as fear and anxiety. It is a risky activity because it calls into question accepted conceptual boundaries, threatening integrity by allowing the Other into the self. Yet this very act is also the source of the ambivalent pleasure that may be experienced in allowing these boundaries, at least for a time, to be disrupted, blurred or crossed. The power of the culturally forbidden and the contaminated provides the opportunity for frissons of exhilaration and heightened sensibility that go beyond the excitement afforded by merely engaging in 'dangerous' activities.

CONCLUDING COMMENTS

In a world in which self-containment and self-regulation are highly valued and encouraged, participation in activities that are culturally coded as 'risky' allows the contemporary body/self to revel, at least for a time, in the pleasures of the 'grotesque' or 'uncivilized' body. In some social contexts, risk-taking is actively encouraged as a means of escaping from the bounds of everyday life, achieving self-actualization, demonstrating the ability to go beyond expectations or performing gender. The thrills and excitement of the carnivalesque have shifted in location from the religious festival to sites such as the seaside resort, the music festival, the fun fair and theme park, the adventure holiday and the 'extreme sport'. Activities such as drug taking and sex provide routes by which the culturally forbidden may be indulged in, at least for a time. The popular media also afford the opportunity to engage vicariously in transgression, to enjoy the sights and sounds of 'grotesque' bodies and thereby experience heightened emotions. Engagement with the marginalized Other is also a potent source of fascination and desire, often at the unconscious level. The courting of symbolic risk implicated by the crossing or blurring of boundaries is a central aspect of the pleasure and excitement associated with transgression and contact with Otherness.

GLOSSARY

Abject: that which provokes feelings of disquiet, disgust, horror and also fascination, which one seeks to expel from one's body and Self as part of maintaining a sense of autonomy, purity and individuation.

Assemblage: the dynamic body/self configured by the interaction of an individual's body with a range of heterogeneous elements, including other bodies, non-human living organisms, material objects, *discourses*, practices, space and place.

Biophilosophical: a term used to encompass philosophical approaches directed at understanding the contingencies and dynamic nature of bodies.

Biopolitics: the disciplining and monitoring of individuals by the state via practices, regulations and *discourses* directed at the body, both at the individual and the population level.

Biopower: the operation of biopolitical power relations through and with the body.

Cosmopolitanism: a word used in Ulrich Beck's writings to denote the social processes occurring inexorably worldwide involving the blurring of boundaries between nation-states and the influence of global processes on these states' politics.

Critical realism: an approach which adopts a weak *social constructionist* perspective by arguing in relation to risk that harmful phenomena exist outside of human perception and understanding but that the ways in which some of these phenomena are identified, named and treated as 'risks' is the product of historical, social, cultural and political processes.

Cultural/symbolic perspective: an approach built upon the writings of Mary Douglas which sees notions of risk as used to establish and maintain conceptual boundaries between Self and *Other*.

Discourse: a defined and coherent way of representing and discussing people, events, ideas or things, as expressed in a range of forums, from everyday talk to the popular media and the internet to expert talk and texts.

Dispositif: a Foucauldian term used to encompass the governing of social problems via a heterogeneous *assemblage* of discursive, administrative, technical, legal, institutional and material elements.

Edgework: a term used to describe voluntary risk-taking activities that challenge and test sociocultural boundaries.

Global citizenship: a new kind of citizenship in which traditional means of defining identity, based on local contexts, are exchanged for a focus on the worldwide perspective.

Globalization: the interconnection of nation-states around the world, so that their social, cultural and economic systems have become progressively influenced by each other.

Governmentality: a theoretical concept drawn from the work of Michel Foucault that addresses the rationalities, techniques and strategies by which subjects are governed and rendered productive in *neo-liberal* societies.

Governmentality perspective: a theoretical approach that uses the *governmentality* literature to understand the role played by risk in the organization and management of societies.

Grid-group: a model developed by Mary Douglas and Aaron Wildavsky to describe the ways in which social structures and cultural values intersect when logics of risk are constructed and expressed.

Habitus: a concept developed by Pierre Bourdieu to describe the set of dispositions and bodily techniques, modes of behaving and deporting oneself, that is passed on from generation to generation and is linked to membership of sub-cultural groups.

Heuristics: perceptual frames or ways of seeing by which people interpret and respond to phenomena such as risk.

Individualization: the breaking down of traditional norms and values that is part of *reflexive modernization*, forcing people to make decisions and choose from a range of options in constructing their life course.

Late modernity: the outcome of broad socio-political and economic changes that have taken place in Western societies since World War II (also referred to by some commentators as 'postmodernity') which have led to a growing sense of the failures of early *modernity* and subsequent uncertainty, ambivalence and distrust of institutions and authorities.

Modernity: the institutions and modes of government and behaviours first established in post-feudal Europe, leading to the development of the industrialized world.

Neo-liberalism: a political approach evident in contemporary Western societies which is characterized by an emphasis on citizens' opportunities to make free choices, albeit guided in certain ways by the state, and which promotes the concept of citizens voluntarily seeking to take responsibility for their own health and welfare.

Normalization: the method by which norms of behaviour or health status are identified, measured and monitored in populations and sub-groups of populations.

Other, the: an individual or member of a social group who is considered radically different from the Self.

Phenomenology: a perspective which is interested in the lived experience of risk and how people construct meanings and knowledges around risks as members of social groups.

Postmodernity: see *late modernity*.

Poststructuralism: a theoretical perspective which is interested in the constitution of bodies, selves and knowledges via language and *discourse* and which emphasizes the contingent, hybrid and performative nature of these phenomena.

Psychoanalytic perspective: an approach that is interested in identifying and analysing the unconscious psychodynamic processes that mediate people's responses to risk, and particularly their emotional responses.

Psychometric: a dominant approach in cognitive psychology that seeks to quantitatively measure the relative influence of different cognitive factors in shaping lay responses to risk.

Reflexive modernization: the criticism of and uncertainty about the outcomes of modernity that have emerged in late modern societies.

Reflexivity: an active response to conditions that arouse fear or anxiety or inspire uncertainty, involving continual assessment of expert claims.

Risk society: the term used by Ulrich Beck to describe a transitional period in late modern societies, incorporating the concept that the processes of modernization have not only produced 'goods' such as wealth and employment but also 'bads': that is, risks.

Risk society perspective: a sociological approach to risk based on Ulrich Beck's writings on *risk society* that draws attention to the macro-sociological processes that are characteristic of late modern societies, including *reflexive modernization* and *individualization*.

Social constructionism: a perspective that sees phenomena such as risks as always knowable and mediated via social and cultural processes rather than as pre-existing objective realities.

Structuralism: an approach in social theory that concentrates on identifying the underlying social structures, hierarchies and cultural categories shaping individuals' experiences, behaviours and beliefs.

Technico-scientific perspective: the perspective on risks common to technical and scientific approaches, which sees risks as objective hazards, threats or dangers that exist and can be measured independently of social and cultural processes.

World risk society: an outcome of *globalization*, in which nation-states are inextricably interconnected with each other and risks therefore cross borders and are shared. Responses to risk must therefore take place at a global rather than national level, involving new alliances and strategies.

REFERENCES

Adams, J. (1995) *Risk*. London: UCL Press.

Aitken, S. (2012) Young men's violence and spaces of addiction: opening up the locker room. *Social & Cultural Geography*, 13(2), 127–43.

Alexander, J. (1996) Critical reflections on 'reflexive modernization'. *Theory, Culture & Society*, 13(4), 133–8.

Althaus, C. (2005) A disciplinary perspective on the epistemological status of risk. *Risk Analysis*, 25(3), 567–88.

Anderson, A. (2006) Media and risk. In Mythen, G. and Walklate, S. (eds), *Beyond the Risk Society: Critical Reflections on Risk and Human Security*. Maidenhead: Open University Press, pp. 114–31.

Anderson, B. (2010) Preemption, precaution, preparedness: anticipatory action and future geographies. *Progress in Human Geography*, 34(6), 777–98.

Anderson, K. (1996) Engendering race research: unsettling the self-Other dichotomy. In Duncan, N. (ed.), *BodySpace*. London: Routledge, pp. 197–211.

Aradau, C. and van Munster, R. (2007) Governing terrorism through risk: taking precautions, (un)knowing the future. *European Journal of International Relations*, 31(1), 89–115.

—— (2012) The time/space of preparedness: anticipating the 'next terrorist attack'. *Space and Culture*, 15(2), 98–109.

Bachelor, S. (2007) 'Getting mad wi' it': risk seeking by young women. In Hannah-Moffat, K. and O'Malley, P. (eds), *Gendered Risks*. London: Routledge-Cavendish, pp. 205–28.

Bakhtin, M. (1984) *Rabelais and His World*. Cambridge, MA: MIT Press.

Barron, M. and Bradford, S. (2007) Corporeal controls: violence, bodies, and young gay men's identities. *Youth & Society*, 39(2), 232–61.

Bauman, Z. (1991) *Modernity and Ambivalence*. Cambridge: Polity Press.

—— (1995) Making and unmaking of strangers. *Thesis Eleven*, 43(1), 1–16.

Beck, U. (1992a) From industrial society to the risk society: questions of survival, social structure and ecological environment. *Theory, Culture & Society*, 9(1), 97–123.

—— (1992b) *Risk Society: Towards a New Modernity*. London: Sage.

—— (1994) The reinvention of politics: towards a theory of reflexive modernization. In Beck, U., Giddens, A. and Lash, S., *Reflexive Modernization: Politics, Tradition and Aesthetics in the Modern Social Order*. Cambridge: Polity Press, pp. 1–55.

—— (1995) *Ecological Politics in the Age of Risk*. Cambridge: Polity Press.

—— (1996a) World risk society as cosmopolitan society? Ecological questions in a framework of manufactured uncertainties. *Theory, Culture & Society*, 13(4), 1–32.

—— (1996b) Risk society and the provident state. In Lash, S., Szerszinski, B. and Wynne, B. (eds), *Risk, Environment and Modernity: Towards a New Ecology*. London: Sage, pp. 27–43.

—— (1999) *World Risk Society*. Cambridge: Polity Press.

—— (2002) The cosmopolitan society and its enemies. *Theory, Culture & Society*, 19(1–2), 17–44.

—— (2006) *The Cosmopolitan Vision*. Cambridge: Polity Press.

—— (2009a) *World at Risk*. Cambridge: Polity Press.

—— (2009b) Critical theory of world risk society: a cosmopolitan vision. *Constellations*, 16(1), 3–22.

—— (2011) Cosmopolitanism as imagined communities of global risk. *American Behavioral Scientist*, 55(10), 1346–61.

—— (2012) Redefining the sociological project: the cosmopolitan challenge. *Sociology*, 46(1), 7–12.

Beck, U. and Beck-Gernsheim, E. (1995) *The Normal Chaos of Love*. Cambridge: Polity Press.

Beck, U. and Grande, E. (2010) Varieties of second modernity: the cosmopolitan turn in social and political theory and research. *The British Journal of Sociology*, 61(3), 409–43.

Bhabha, H. (1994) *The Location of Culture*. London: Routledge.

Binkley, S. (2009) Governmentality, temporality and practice: from the individualization of risk to the 'contradictory movements of the soul'. *Time & Society*, 18(1), 86–105.

Bloor, M. (1995) *The Sociology of HIV Transmission*. London: Sage.

Boholm, M. (2012) The semantic distinction between 'risk' and 'danger': a linguistic analysis. *Risk Analysis*, 32(2), 281–93.

Bourdieu, P. (1984) *Distinction: A Social Critique of the Judgement of Taste*. London: Routledge & Kegan Paul.

Bradbury, J. (1989) The policy implications of differing concepts of risk. *Science, Technology & Human Values*, 14(4), 380–99.

Brooks, A. (2008) Reconceptualizing reflexivity and dissonance in professional and personal domains. *The British Journal of Sociology*, 59(3), 539–59.

Brown, J. (ed.) (1989) *Environmental Threats: Perception, Analysis and Management*. London: Belhaven Press, pp. 48–66.

Brymer, E. and Schweitzer, R. (2012) Extreme sports are good for your health: a phenomenological understanding of fear and anxiety in extreme sport. *Journal of Health Psychology*, in press, corrected proof available online.

Bunton, R. and Coveney, J. (2011) Drugs' pleasures. *Critical Public Health*, 21(1), 9–24.

Burke, P. (1994) *Popular Culture in Early Modern Europe*, second rev. edn. Aldershot: Scolar Press.

Busby, J. and Duckett, D. (2012) Social risk amplification as an attribution: the case of zoonotic disease outbreaks. *Journal of Risk Research*, 15(9), 1049–74.

Casey, R., Goudie, R. and Reeve, K. (2008) Homeless women in public spaces: strategies of resistance. *Housing Studies*, 23(6), 899–916.

Castel, R. (1991) From dangerousness to risk. In Burchell, C., Gordon, C. and Miller, P. (eds), *The Foucault Effect: Studies in Governmentality*. London: Harvester/Wheatsheaf, pp. 281–98.

Castree, N. (2010) *The Politics of Climate Change* by Anthony Giddens (book review). *The Sociological Review*, 58(1), 156–62.

Catellier, J. Allen and Yang, Z. (2012) Trust and affect: how do they impact risk information seeking in a health context? *Journal of Risk Research*, 15(8), 891–911.

Cohen, S. and Taylor, L. (1976/1992) *Escape Attempts: The Theory and Practice of Resistance to Everyday Life*, second rev. edn. London: Routledge.

Collison, M. (1996) In search of the high life: drugs, crime, masculinities and consumption. *British Journal of Criminology*, 36(3) 428–44.

Comaroff, J. (1993) The diseased heart of Africa: medicine, colonialism, and the black body. In Lindenbaum, S. and Lock, M. (eds), *Knowledge, Power and Practice: The Anthropology of Medicine and Everyday Life*. Berkeley, CA: University of California Press, pp. 305–29.

Davidson, J. and Milligan, C. (2004) Embodying emotion sensing space: introducing emotional geographies. *Social & Cultural Geography*, 5(4), 523–32.

Davison, C., Frankel, S. and Davey Smith, G. (1992) The limits of lifestyle: re-assessing 'fatalism' in the popular culture of illness prevention. *Social Science and Medicine*, 34(6), 675–85.

Dean, M. (1997) Sociology after society. In Owen, D. (ed.), *Sociology after Postmodernism*. London: Sage, pp. 205–28.

—— (1999) Risk, calculable and incalculable. In Lupton, D. (ed.), *Risk and Sociocultural Theory: New Directions and Perspectives*. Cambridge: Cambridge University Press, pp. 131–59.

—— (2007) *Governing Societies: Political Perspectives on Domestic and International Rule*. Milton Keynes: Open University Press.

—— (2010) Power at the heart of the present: exception, risk and sovereignty. *European Journal of Cultural Studies*, 13(4), 459–75.

Dennis, S. (2011) Smoking causes creative responses: on state antismoking policy and resilient habits. *Critical Public Health*, 21(1), 25–35.

Docter, S., Street, J., Braunack-Mayer, A. and van der Wilt, G.-J. (2011) Public perceptions of pandemic influenza resource allocation: a deliberate forum using grid/group analysis. *Journal of Public Health Policy*, 32(3), 350–66.

Dohle, S., Keller, C. and Siegrist, M. (2012) Fear and anger: antecedents and consequences of emotional responses to mobile communication. *Journal of Risk Research*, 15(4), 435–46.

Douglas, M. (1966/1969) *Purity and Danger: An Analysis of Concepts of Pollution and Taboo*. London: Routledge & Kegan Paul.

—— (1985) *Risk Acceptability According to the Social Sciences*. New York: Russell Sage Foundation.

—— (1992) *Risk and Blame: Essays in Cultural Theory*. London: Routledge.

Douglas, M. and Wildavsky, A. (1982) *Risk and Culture: An Essay on the Selection of Technological and Environmental Dangers*. Berkeley, CA: University of California Press.

Drake, F. (2011) Protesting mobile phone masts: risk, neoliberalism, and governmentality. *Science, Technology & Human Values*, 36(4), 522–48.

Duncan, N. (1996) Renegotiating gender and sexuality in public and private spaces. In Duncan, N. (ed.), *BodySpace*. London: Routledge, pp. 127–45.

Edelman, E.A. (2011) 'This area has been declared a Prostitution Free Zone': discursive formations of space, the state, and trans 'sex worker' bodies. *Journal of Homosexuality*, 58(6/7), 848–64.

Elias, N. (1939/1994) *The Civilizing Process*. Oxford: Blackwell.

Ewald, F. (1991) Insurance and risks. In Burchell, C., Cordon, C. and Miller, P. (eds), *The Foucault Effect: Studies in Governmentality*. London: Harvester/Wheatsheaf, pp. 197–210.

—— (1993) Two infinities of risk. In Massumi, B. (ed.), *The Politics of Everyday Fear*. Minneapolis, MN: University of Minnesota Press, pp. 221–8.

Featherstone, M. (1995) *Undoing Culture: Globalization, Postmodernism and Identity*. London: Sage.

Ferguson, H. (1997) Me and my shadows: on the accumulation of body-images in Western society. Part one – the image and the image of the body in pre-modern society. *Body & Society*, 3(3), 1–32.

Fischer, P., Vingilis, E., Greitemeyer, T. and Vogrincic, C. (2011) Risk-taking and the media. *Risk Analysis*, 31(5), 699–705.

Fleming, P., Townsend, E., van Hilten, J., Spence, A. and Ferguson, E. (2012) Expert relevance and the use of context-specific heuristic processes in risk perception. *Journal of Risk Research*, 15(7), 857–73.

Foucault, M. (1984) The politics of health in the eighteenth century. In Rabinow, P. (ed.), *The Foucault Reader*. New York: Pantheon Books, pp. 273–89.

—— (1988) Technologies of the self. In Martin, L., Gutman, H. and Hutton, P. (eds), *Technologies of the Self: A Seminar with Michel Foucault*. London: Tavistock, pp. 16–49.

—— (1991) Governmentality. In Burchell, G., Gordon, C. and Miller, P. (eds), *The Foucault Effect: Studies in Governmentality*. Hemel Hempstead: Harvester Wheatsheaf, pp. 87–104.

Fox, N. (1999) Postmodern reflections on 'risks', 'hazards' and life choices. In Lupton, D. (ed.), *Risk and Sociocultural Theory: New Directions and Perspectives*. Cambridge: Cambridge University Press, pp. 12-33.

—— (2002) What a 'risky' body can do: why people's health choices are not all based in evidence. *Health Education Journal*, 61(2), 166–79.

—— (2011) The ill-health assemblage: beyond the body-with-organs. *Health Sociology Review*, 20(4), 359–71.

Gailey, J. (2009) 'Starving is the most fun a girl could have': the pro-ana subculture as edgework. *Critical Criminology*, 17(2), 93–108.

Gard, M. (2011) *The End of the Obesity Epidemic*. London: Routledge.

Gard, M. and Wright, J. (2005) *The Obesity Epidemic: Science, Morality and Ideology*, London: Routledge.

Gerber, D., Burton-Jeangros, C. and Dubied, A. (2011) Animals in the media: new boundaries of risk? *Health, Risk & Society*, 13(1), 17–30.

Giddens, A. (1990) *The Consequences of Modernity*. Cambridge: Polity Press.

—— (1991) *Modernity and Self-Identity*. Cambridge: Polity Press.

—— (1992) *The Transformation of Intimacy: Sexuality, Love and Eroticism in Modern Societies*. Cambridge: Polity Press.

—— (1994) Living in a post-traditional society. In Beck, U., Giddens, A. and Lash, S., *Reflexive Modernization: Politics, Tradition and Aesthetics in the Modern Social Order*. Cambridge: Polity Press, pp. 56–109.

—— (1998) Risk society: the context of British politics. In Franklin, J. (ed.), *The Politics of Risk Society*. Cambridge: Polity Press, pp. 23–34.

Giddens, A. (2003) *Runaway World: How Globalization Is Reshaping Our Lives*, 2nd edn. New York: Routledge.

—— (2005) Scaring people may be the only way to avoid the new-style risks of global terrorism. *New Statesman*, 18(841), 29.

—— (2011) *The Politics of Climate Change*, 2nd edn. Cambridge: Polity Press.

Gordon, C. (1991) Governmental rationality: an introduction. In Burchell, G., Gordon, C. and Miller, P. (eds), *The Foucault Effect: Studies in Governmentality*. Hemel Hempstead: Harvester Wheatsheaf, pp. 1–52.

Gordon, N. and Filc, D. (2005) Hamas and the destruction of risk society. *Constellations*, 12(4), 542–60.

Gotfrit, L. (1991) Women dancing back: disruption and the politics of pleasure. In Giroux, H. (ed.), *Postmodernism, Feminism, and Cultural Politics: Redrawing Educational Boundaries*. Albany, NY: State University of New York Press, pp. 174–95.

Greco, M. (1993) Psychosomatic subjects and the 'duty to be well': personal agency within medical rationality. *Economy and Society*, 22(3), 357–72.

Green, E. and Singleton, C. (2006) Risky bodies at leisure: young women negotiating space and place. *Sociology*, 40(5), 853–71.

Green, J. (1997) Risk and the construction of social identity: children's talk about accidents. *Sociology of Health & Illness*, 19(4), 457–79.

Greenberg, M., Haas, C., Cox Jr., A., Lowrie, K., McComas, K. and North, W. (2012) Ten most important accomplishments in risk analysis. *Risk Analysis*, 32(5), 771–81.

Grosz, E. (1994) *Volatile Bodies: Toward a Corporeal Feminism*. Sydney: Allen & Unwin.

Hacking, I. (1990) *The Taming of Chance*. Cambridge: Cambridge University Press.

Hall, S. (1997) The work of representation. In Hall, S. (ed.), *Representation: Cultural Representations and Signifying Practices*. London: Sage, pp. 13–74.

Hannah-Moffat, K. and O'Malley, P. (2007) Gendered risks: an introduction. In Hannah-Moffat, K. and O'Malley, P. (eds), *Gendered Risks*. London: Routledge-Cavendish, pp. 1–29.

Hart, G. and Boulton, M. (1995) Sexual behaviour in gay men: towards a sociology of risk. In Aggleton, P., Davies, P. and

Hart, G. (eds), *AIDS: Safety, Sexuality and Risk*. London: Taylor & Francis, pp. 55–67.

Hier, S. (2004) Risky spaces and dangerous faces: urban surveillance, social disorder and CCTV. *Social & Legal Studies*, 13(4), 541–54.

Hilgartner, S. (1992) The social construction of risk objects: or, how to pry open networks of risk. In Short, J. and Clarke, L. (eds), *Organizations, Uncertainties, and Risk*. Boulder, CO: Westview Press, pp. 39–53.

Hindmoor, A. (2010) The banking crisis: grid, group and the state of the debate. *Australian Journal of Public Administration*, 69(4), 442–56.

Houston, S. (2001) Transcending the fissure in risk theory: critical realism and child welfare. *Child and Family Social Work*, 6(3), 219–28.

Hughes, E., Kitzinger, J. and Murdock, G. (2006) The media and risk. In Taylor-Gooby, P. and Zinn, J. (eds), *Risk in Social Science*. Oxford: Oxford University Press, pp. 250–70.

Hunter, I. (1993) Subjectivity and government. *Economy and Society*, 22(1), 123–34.

Jackson, J. (2006) Introducing fear of crime to risk research. *Risk Analysis*, 26(1), 253–64.

Jayne, M., Valentine, G. and Holloway, S. (2010) Emotional, embodied and affective geographies of alcohol, drinking and drunkenness. *Transactions of the Institute of British Geographers*, 35(4), 540–54.

Jensen, M. and Blok, A. (2008) Pesticides in the risk society: the view from everyday life. *Current Sociology*, 56(5), 757–78.

Jette, S., Wilson, B. and Sparks, R. (2007) Female youths' perceptions of smoking in popular films. *Qualitative Health Research*, 17(3), 323–39.

Kaprow, M. (1985) Manufacturing danger: fear and pollution in industrial society. *American Anthropology*, 87, 342–56.

Kemshall, H. (1997) Sleep safely: crime risks may be smaller than you think. *Social Policy & Administration*, 31(3), 247–59.

Kendall, G. and Wickham, G. (1992) Health and the social body. In Scott, S., Williams, G., Platt, S. and Thomas, H. (eds), *Private Risks and Public Dangers*. Aldershot: Avebury, pp. 8–18.

Kent, L. (2001) Fighting abjection: representing fat women. In Braziel, J. and LeBesco, K. (eds), *Bodies Out of Bounds: Fatness and Transgression*, Berkeley, CA: University of California Press, pp. 130–50.

Kristeva, J. (1982) *Powers of Horror: An Essay on Abjection*. New York: Columbia University Press.

Kroker, A. and Kroker, M. (1988) Panic sex in America. In Kroker, A. and Kroker, M. (eds), *Body Invaders: Sexuality and the Postmodern Condition*. Toronto: Macmillan.

Lash, S. (1993) Reflexive modernization: the aesthetic dimension. *Theory, Culture & Society*, 10(1), 1–23.

—— (1994) Reflexivity and its doubles: structure, aesthetics, community. In Beck, U., Giddens, A. and Lash, S., *Reflexive Modernization: Politics, Tradition and Aesthetics in the Modern Social Order*. Cambridge: Polity Press, pp. 110–73.

—— (2000) Risk culture. In Adam, B., Beck, U. and van Loon, J. (eds), *The Risk Society and Beyond: Critical Issues for Social Theory*. London: Sage, pp. 47–62.

Lash, S. and Urry, J. (1994) *Economies of Signs and Space*. London: Sage.

Lash, S. and Wynne, B. (1992) Introduction. In Beck, U., *Risk Society: Towards a New Modernity*. London: Sage, pp. 1–8.

Leaker, M. and Dunk-West, P. (2011) Socio-cultural risk? Reporting on a qualitative study with female street-based sex workers. *Sociological Research Online*, 16(4). Online. Available at: http://www.socresonline.org.uk/16/4/9.html (accessed 4 March 2012).

Lees, L. and Baxter, R. (2011) A 'building event' of fear: thinking through the geography of architecture. *Social & Cultural Geography*, 12(2), 107–22.

Lewis, J. and Bennett, F. (2003) Themed issue on gender and individualisation. *Social Policy & Society*, 3(1), 43–5.

Lippert, R. and Stenson, K. (2010) Advancing governmentality studies: lessons from social constructionism. *Theoretical Criminology*, 14(4), 473–94.

Llewellyn, D. (2008) The psychology of risk taking: towards the integration of psychometric and neuropsychological paradigms. *The American Journal of Psychology*, 121(3), 363–76.

Lois, J. (2005) Gender and emotion management in the stages of edgework. In Lyng, S. (ed.), *Edgework: The Sociology of Risk-Taking*. New York: Routledge, pp. 117–52.

Luhmann, N. (1993) *Risk: A Sociological Theory*. New York: Aldine de Gruyter.

Lupton, D. (1995) *The Imperative of Health: Public Health and the Regulated Body*. London: Sage.

—— (1998) *The Emotional Self: A Sociocultural Exploration*. London: Sage.

—— (1999) Dangerous places and the unpredictable stranger: constructions of fear of crime. *Australian & New Zealand Journal of Criminology*, 32(1), 1–15.

—— (2012a) M-health and health promotion: the digital cyborg and surveillance society. *Social Theory & Health*, 10(3), 229–44.

—— (2012b) 'Precious cargo': foetal subjects and reproductive citizenship. *Critical Public Health*, 22(3), 329–40.

—— (2012c) *Fat*. London: Routledge.

Lupton, D. and Tulloch, J. (2002a) 'Life would be pretty dull without risk': voluntary risk-taking and its pleasures. *Health, Risk & Society*, 4(2), 113–24.

—— (2002b) 'Risk is a part of your life': risk epistemologies among a group of Australians. *Sociology*, 36(2), 317–34.

Lyng, S. (1990) Edgework: a social psychological analysis of voluntary risk taking. *American Journal of Sociology*, 95(4), 851–86.

—— (2005) Edgework and the risk-taking experience. In Lyng, S. (ed.), *Edgework: The Sociology of Risk-Taking*. New York: Routledge, pp. 17–49.

—— (2008) Edgework, risk, and uncertainty. In Zinn, J. (ed.), *Social Theories of Risk and Uncertainty: An Introduction*. Oxford: Blackwell Publishing, pp. 106–37.

Lyng, S. and Matthews, R. (2007) Risk, edgework, and masculinities. In Hannah-Moffat, K. and O'Malley, P. (eds), *Gendered Risks*. London: Routledge-Cavendish, pp. 75–98.

Macgill, S. (1989) Risk perception and the public: insights from research around Sellafield. In Brown, J. (ed.), *Environmental Threats: Perception, Analysis and Management*. London: Belhaven Press, pp. 48–66.

MacLean, S. (2008) Volatile bodies: stories of corporeal pleasure and damage in marginalised young people's drug use. *International Journal of Drug Policy*, 19(5), 375–83.

Maffesoli, M. (1996) *The Time of the Tribes: The Decline of Individualism in Mass Society*. London: Sage.

Mairal, G. (2011) The history and narrative of risk in the media. *Health, Risk & Society*, 13(1), 65–79.

Martell, L. (2009) Global inequality, human rights and power: a critique of Ulrich Beck's cosmopolitanism. *Critical Sociology*, 35(2), 253–72.

Martin, E. (1994) *Flexible Bodies: Tracking Immunity in American Culture From the Days of Polio to the Age of AIDS*. Boston, MA: Beacon Press.

Massumi, B. (1993) Everywhere you want to be: introduction to fear. In Massumi, B. (ed.), *The Politics of Everyday Fear*. Minneapolis, MN: University of Minnesota Press, pp. 3–38.

Masuda, J. and Garvin, T. (2006) Place, culture, and the social amplification of risk. *Risk Analysis*, 26(2), 437–54.

Maticka-Tyndale, E. (1992) Social construction of HIV transmission and prevention among heterosexual young adults. *Social Problems*, 39(3), 238–52.

McGinn, C. (2011) *The Meaning of Disgust*. New York: Oxford University Press.

Mellor, P. and Shilling, C. (1997) *Re-forming the Body: Religion, Community and Modernity*. London: Sage.

Melucci, A. (1996) *The Playing Self: Person and Meaning in the Planetary Society*. Cambridge: Cambridge University Press.

Merleau-Ponty, M. (1962) *Phenomenology of Perception*. London: Routledge & Kegan Paul.

Michael, M. (1996) *Constructing Identities: the Social, the Nonhuman and Change*. London: Sage.

Miller, T. (2010) My global financial crisis. *Journal of Communication Inquiry*, 34(4), 432–8.

Miller, W. (1997) *The Anatomy of Disgust*. Cambridge, MA: Harvard University Press.

Mossman, D. (1997) Deinstitutionalization, homelessness, and the myth of psychiatric abandonment: a structural anthropology perspective. *Social Science & Medicine*, 44(1), 71–84.

Muchembled, R. (1985) *Popular Culture and Elite Culture in France, 1400–1750*. Baton Rouge, LA: Louisiana State University Press.

Mulinari, D. and Sandell, K. (2009) A feminist re-reading of theories of late modernity: Beck, Giddens, and the location of gender. *Critical Sociology*, 35(4), 493–507.

Myslik, W. (1996) Renegotiating the social/sexual identities of places: gay communities as safe havens or sites of resistance? In Duncan, N. (ed.), *BodySpace*. London: Routledge, pp. 156–69.

Mythen, G. (2007) Reappraising the risk society thesis: telescopic sight or myopic vision? *Current Sociology*, 55(6), 793–813.

Nayak, A. (1997) Frozen bodies: disclosing whiteness in Haagen-Dazs advertising. *Body & Society*, 3(3), 51–72.

Nerlich, B. and Halliday, C. (2007) Avian flu: the creation of expectations in the interplay between science and the media. *Sociology of Health & Illness*, 29(1), 46–65.

Newmahr, S. (2011) Chaos, order, and collaboration: toward a feminist conceptualization of edgework. *Journal of Contemporary Ethnography*, 40(6), 682–712.

Oels, A. (2011) Rendering climate change governable by risk: from probability to contingency. *Geoforum*, in press, corrected proof available online.

Olofsson, A. and Ohman, S. (2007) Views of risk in Sweden: global fatalism and local control. An empirical investigation of Ulrich Beck's theory of new risks. *Journal of Risk Research*, 10(2), 177–96.

Olofsson, A. and Rashid, S. (2011) The white (male) effect and risk perception: can equality make a difference? *Risk Analysis*, 31(6), 1016–32.

Olstead, R. (2011) Gender, space and fear: a study of women's edgework. *Emotion, Space and Society*, 4(2), 86–94.

O'Malley, P. (1992) Risk, power and crime prevention. *Economy and Society*, 21(3), 252–75.

Perin, C. (1988) *Belonging in America: Reading Between the Lines*. Madison, WI: The University of Wisconsin Press.

Rasborg, K. (2012) '(World) risk society' or 'new rationalities of risk'? A critical discussion of Ulrich Beck's theory of reflexive modernity. *Thesis Eleven*, 108(1), 3–25.

Reddy, S. (1996) Claims to expert knowledge and the subversion of democracy: the triumph of risk over uncertainty. *Economy and Society*, 25(2), 222–54.

Rhodes, T. (1995) Theorizing and researching 'risk': notes on the social relations of risk in heroin users' lifestyles. In Aggleton, P., Davies, P. and Hart, G. (eds), *AIDS: Safety, Sexuality and Risk*. London: Taylor & Francis, pp. 125–43.

Rich, E., Evans, J. and De Pian, L. (2011) Children's bodies, surveillance and the obesity crisis. In Rich, E., Monaghan, L. and Aphramor, L. (eds), *Debating Obesity: Critical Perspectives*. London: Palgrave Macmillan, pp. 139–63.

Rigakos, G. and Law, A. (2009) Risk, realism and the politics of resistance. *Critical Sociology*, 35(1), 79–103.

Rose, G. (1993) *Feminism and Geography: The Limits of Geographical Knowledge*. Minneapolis, MN: University of Minnesota Press.

Royal Society (1992) *Risk: Analysis, Perception and Management*. London: Royal Society.

Said, E. (1978) *Orientalism*. London: Penguin.

Salter, M. and Mutlu, C. (2011) Psychoanalytic theory and border control. *European Journal of Social Theory*, 15(2), 179–95.

Schubart, R. (1995) From desire to deconstruction: horror films and audience reactions. In Kidd-Hewitt, D. and Osborne, R. (eds), *Crime and the Media: The Postmodern Spectacle*. London: Pluto, pp. 219–42.

Scott, J., Carrington, K. and McIntosh, A. (2011) Established-outsider relations and fear of crime in mining towns. *Sociologia Ruralis*, 52(2), 147–69.

Shildrick. M. (2007) Dangerous discourses: anxiety, desire and disability. *Studies in Gender and Sexuality*, 8(3), 221–44.

Short, J. (1984) The social fabric at risk: toward the social transformation of risk analysis. *American Sociological Review*, 49(6), 711–25.

Sibley, D. (1995) *Geographies of Exclusion: Society and Difference in the West*. London: Routledge.

Siegrist, M., Keller, C. and Kiers, H. (2005) A new look at the psychometric paradigm of perception of hazards. *Risk Analysis*, 25(1), 211–22.

Skolbekken, J.-A. (1995) The risk epidemic in medical journals. *Social Science & Medicine*, 40(3), 291–305.

Slovic, P. (1987) Perception of risk. *Science*, 236(4812), 280–5.

Smart, B. (1993) *Postmodernity*. London: Routledge.

Smith, C. (2005) Financial edgework: trading in market currents. In Lyng, S. (ed.), *Edgework: The Sociology of Risk-Taking*. New York: Routledge, pp. 187–200.

Smith, N., Cebulla, A., Cox, L. and Davies, A. (2006) Risk perception and the presentation of self: reflections on fieldwork on risk. *Forum: Qualitative Social Research*, 7(1). Online. Available at: http:www.qualitative-research.net/index.php/fqs/article/view/54 (accessed 7 May 2012).

Stallybrass, P. and White, A. (1986) *The Politics and Poetics of Transgression*. Ithaca, NY: Cornell University Press.

Stoddart, M. and MacDonald, L. (2011) 'Keep it wild, keep it local': comparing news media and the internet as sites for environmental movement activism for Jumbo Pass, British Columbia. *Canadian Journal of Sociology*, 36(4), 313–35.

Szerszinski, B., Lash, S. and Wynne, B. (1996) Introduction: ecology, realism and the social sciences. In Lash, S., Szerszinski, B. and Wynne, B. (eds), *Risk, Environment and Modernity: Towards a New Ecology*. London: Sage, pp. 1–26.

Tatarchevskiy, T. (2011) The 'popular' culture of internet activism. *New Media & Society*, 13(2), 297–313.

Taylor-Gooby, P. and Zinn, J. (2006) Current directions in risk research: new developments in psychology and sociology. *Risk Analysis*, 26(2), 397–411.

Thompson, H. (1972) *Fear and Loathing in Las Vegas*. New York: Random House.

Thomson, R. (1997) *Extraordinary Bodies: Figuring Physical Disability in American Culture and Literature*. New York: Columbia University Press.

Tudor, A. (1995) Unruly bodies, unquiet minds. *Body & Society*, 1(1), 25–42.

Tulloch, J. (2006) *One Day in July: Experiencing 7/7*. London: Little Brown.

—— (2008a) Culture and risk. In Zinn, J. (ed.), *Social Theories of Risk and Uncertainty: An Introduction*. Oxford: Blackwell Publishing, pp. 138–67.

—— (2008b) Risk and subjectivity: experiencing terror. *Health, Risk & Society*, 10(5), 451–65.

Tulloch, J. and Lupton, D. (2003) *Risk and Everyday Life*. London: Sage.

Valentine, G. (1996) (Re)negotiating the 'heterosexual street': lesbian productions of space. In Duncan, N. (ed.), *BodySpace*. London: Routledge, pp. 146–55.

Valentine, K. and Fraser, S. (2008) Trauma, damage and pleasure: rethinking problematic drug use. *International Journal of Drug Policy*, 19(5), 410–16.

van Loon, J. (2002) *Risk and Technological Culture: Towards a Sociology of Virulence*. London: Routledge.

Vaughan, B. (2002) Cultured punishments: the promise of grid-group theory. *Theoretical Criminology*, 6(4), 411–31.

Washer, P. (2006) Representations of mad cow disease. *Social Science & Medicine*, 62(2), 457–66.

Whittaker, D. and Hart, G. (1996) Research note: managing risks: the social organization of indoor sex work. *Sociology of Health & Illness*, 18(3), 399–414.

Whitzman, C. (2007) Stuck at the front door: gender, fear of crime and the challenge of creating safer space. *Environment and Planning A*, 39(11), 2715–32.

Wild, L. (2005) Transgressive terrain: risk, otherness and 'new age' nomadism. In Watson, S. and Moran, A. (eds), *Trust, Risk and Uncertainty*. Houndmills: Palgrave Macmillan, pp. 181–202.

Wilkinson, I. (2006) Health, risk and 'social suffering'. *Health, Risk & Society*, 8(1), 1–8.

Willig, C. (2008) A phenomenological investigation of the experience of taking part in 'extreme sports'. *Journal of Health Psychology*, 13(5), 690–702.

Wynne, B. (1989) Frameworks of rationality in risk management: towards the testing of naive sociology. In Brown, J. (ed.), *Environmental Threats: Perception, Analysis and Management*. London: Belhaven Press, pp. 33–47.

—— (1996) May the sheep safely graze? A reflexive view of the expert-lay knowledge divide. In Lash, S., Szerszinski, B. and Wynne, B. (eds), *Risk, Environment and Modernity: Towards a New Ecology*. London: Sage, pp. 44–83.

Young, R. (1995) *Colonial Desire: Hybridity in Theory, Culture and Race*. London: Routledge.

INDEX